SUDDEN STRANGERS

AARON and WALTER FRICKE

SUDDEN STRANGERS

The Story of a Gay Son and His Father

St. Martin's Press / New York

Design by Judith A. Stagnitto

Library of Congress Cataloging-in-Publication Data

Fricke, Aaron.
    Sudden strangers : the story of a gay son and his father /
Aaron and Walter Fricke.
        p.   cm.
    ISBN 0-312-05869-1
        1. Fricke, Aaron.   2. Fricke, Walter.   3. Fathers and sons—
United States.   4. Gay men—United States—Biography.
    I. Fricke, Walter.   II. Title.
    HQ76.3.U5F75   1991
    306.874'2'092—dc20   90-27344
                                                              CIP

First Edition: May 1991
10 9 8 7 6 5 4 3 2 1

To Lauretta and Marian

CONTENTS

INTRODUCTION

This is a story about Walter Fricke and Aaron Fricke, father and son, heterosexual and gay (respectively on all counts).

The first question you are bound to ask about a book written by a heterosexual father and a gay son is, "What about the wife and mother; why wasn't she included?" My parents have been divorced for nine years, but that is not why my mother has not contributed to this book. Between my dad and me, there have been many dramatic conflicts to overcome; but between my mom and me, there have been no major struggles. My relationship with my mother would be better suited to a different kind of book—a recipe book, perhaps.

It has taken six years to complete this book. During that time, there were periods when it was worked on steadily and times when the material was abandoned as hopeless. The book changed as our father/son relationship changed, and each transformation of the book reflected the transformations in our relationship. It is neither the same book nor the same

My dad sailing through the Panama Canal when he was thirty-three.

relationship that we started with six years ago. This was a book that had to be lived, not simply written.

The final product is the story of an evolving father/son relationship, a story of two people with different ways of looking at the world, and of the hurdles we needed to overcome to respect each other.

SUDDEN STRANGERS

UNDERSTANDING
THE PAST

When I was a little boy, my dad would take me to work with him every so often. Going to work with one's father might be boring for a lot of kids, but it wasn't for me. My father's job as a ship's pilot had him navigating large freighters into New England and New York City ports. So when I went to work with him, I was boarding huge supertankers twelve stories high and two and a half football fields long.

There were a few rules my father set for me on these trips: I could not touch any instruments on the bridge; I could walk but not run anywhere I wanted on the deck; and most importantly, when he raised his hand, it meant he was engaged in some precise maneuvering of the ship and there was to be no talking or distractions. Usually, I knew intuitively to stay in the background, but on those occasions when his quiet, professional intensity went unnoticed and I chimed up with some question or other, his hand shot up and abruptly stopped me in mid-inquiry. Later on, when he was finished, he would ask me what it was I had wanted to know or say. I could rarely remember. What I do remember is that effort he made to retract any discouragement with which he might have dampened my curiosity. He always took pains to let me know that asking questions was the right thing to do—just not while he was at the helm of a fifty-thousand-ton piece of machinery.

One time when I was fourteen, my dad decided to take me along on one of his piloting jobs to New York City. I looked forward to spending the time with him and some time in the city, too. As we sailed down the East River, I looked out at eye level to the tenth story of the buildings we passed. The city itself was enough to inspire awe, but knowing that my dad was in control of this mass of steel sailing by filled me with an overwhelming sense of wonder.

The sea was smooth during our journey—at least I thought it was. I soon learned that what constituted smooth sailing for a supertanker was something a lot choppier for the dinky pilot boat that came to pick us up at Stapleton-Anchorage Point, not too far from the Statue of Liberty. I looked down from the deck at the pilot boat's repeated attempts to get nudged close enough to the tanker so that my father and I could climb the Jacob's ladder down to it. With each attempt, the pilot boat was knocked about in the surf and I was petrified of having to jump from the moderately stationary tanker onto this moving platform. My father was nervous, too, but he told me it was either climb down or stay on board and sail to Brazil with the stinky sailors. I didn't have the guts to tell him just how tempting that prospect was.

He went down first. He said he was going to show me how easy it would be, but I knew he just wanted to be down closer to the water in case he had to rescue me. Then came my turn.

I crept slowly down the side of the ship and followed my father's instructions to look directly ahead while descending. At one point, however, I had to get some bearing on how much more ladder was left before I reached the bottom, so I glanced down and found I had about three more rungs to go. Except for one slight problem: There was only surging ocean below the ladder. The pilot boat had gotten caught in a swell and was tossing in the surf at least one hundred feet away from the tanker. Meanwhile, I was left dangling three-quarters of the way down a fifty-foot-high wall of steel. Obviously, I lived to tell this story. Within five minutes, the pilot boat was positioned under me, and after some coaxing from my dad, I made the four-foot leap from the bottom of the ladder to the safety of his arms.

Adventures like this were part of my dad's daily work routine. Yet as exciting as this kind of work was, I knew I was not going to follow in his footsteps. I was going to seek out my own particular brand of excitement.

Once we got on solid ground, we headed for my paternal grandmother's house in Brooklyn. This house was near the one in which my father had been raised during the Depression. That night, I told my dad that I was thinking about going over to the movies in Manhattan the next day. He said that would be fine, since he had business to take care of at the stock exchange. He woke up and left early the next morning. I woke up later and got myself ready. I had no intention of going to the movies, however; during the entire trip, I had been secretly working up enough guts to go into the city and buy an issue of *Hung Pig* or some such magazine with naked men in it.

I knew the perils of deceiving my father—he had told me himself that one lie leads to another, even bigger lie—but two years earlier I had seen such magazines right out in the open at a news shop on Madison Avenue. Now I was perversely drawn back to the same spot like some kind of gay spawning salmon. For all I knew, this was the only place in the universe with these magazines. With an existential resoluteness, I figured out how to get from Brooklyn to Madison Avenue by subway.

It took me two hours of walking up and down Madison Avenue before I had the courage to enter the shop. My pulse pounded, my palms sweat, and my grace atrophied as I went in, but my method for pulling off this crime against nature had been too extensively premeditated to turn back at that point.

I first picked up a copy of weekly *Variety*, knowing that I would need something to conceal my primary purchase. I took a few steps, glanced skyward, and found that the objects of my desire were still there on the top shelf, just as they had been two years earlier. I indiscriminately grabbed one, placed it on top of the *Variety*, went over to the counter, and, to my relief, bought both of them from a completely disengaged New York cashier. Before even reaching the threshold of the doorway to the shop, I had the magazine tightly wedged between the pages of *Variety*—hidden from view.

The urban rhythms of New York did not exactly allow me to be alone with my guilt (or my porno), but those same rhythms did, at least, give me a chance to carry this guilt anonymously. Or so I thought.

By the freakiest of freak coincidences, my father boarded the same car of the same subway train that I was taking to get back to Brooklyn. Our eyes met instantly, the moment the subway doors opened. I sat there paralyzed with fear as he walked right up to me and tried to initiate a frolicking conversation about the astronomical odds against our running into each other during a one-day visit to the city. I tightened my grasp on *Variety* and looked down to make sure nothing was showing. I was afraid I was going to have a cerebral hemorrhage from stress before we arrived in Brooklyn. At one point, he actually touched my tightly clutched bundle of shame, saying, "Whatchya got?" I milked my adolescent detachment for all it was worth. He just interpreted this combination of fear, anxiety, and detachment as a sign that I was adapting appropriately to New York City. I interpreted the entire scene as an evil omen, so when we arrived at our stop in Brooklyn and he stood up to get off, I stood up behind him but left the porno on the subway seat without ever getting a chance to look at it.

Shortly after this trip to New York with my father, I became emotionally isolated. I retreated into my own world and my morale sank. I turned to food as an emotional escape and my weight shot up to 217½ pounds—all this because I felt remorse for being a homosexual. Remorse can be so debilitating, especially remorse about everything that you are or anything that you will become.

After about two years of that, I met a high school classmate who was openly gay and things started to change. My new friend had everything I needed to help me counter the stifling feelings I had developed. He had a listening ear, he had a shoulder to cry on, and he had gay porno. Through him I met other gay friends, and the feelings of isolation that had engulfed me gradually began to subside, as did my weight.

My dad was unaware of any of this until much later, when he read practically those same words in the book where I had written them, *Reflections of a Rock Lobster*. He had just been going through my teenage years with all the subconscious expectations that parents have for their kids: I'd graduate from high school, I'd go to college, I'd get married, and I'd have kids of my own. He didn't premeditate this as a restrictive parental edict, he just took it for granted. Within this structure, there would be plenty of room for me to make my own choices and then to succeed or fail at them. Barring any accidental death or dismemberment mishap, this "high school, college, marriage, kids" scheme represented the bare bones of my father's most subconscious middle-class, white-collar expectations of me. So it was more than just a shock when, at age eighteen, I told him that I was a homosexual; it was more like an unraveling of his expectations.

Then a few months after that, when I asked for his blessing to sue my high school for the right to take a male date to my senior prom, it was, as he so delicately puts it, "the icing on the cake." He gave me his blessing to do what I felt was right, without offering either his approval or disapproval. It took a lot of strength for him to allow me that freedom, because he knew I would not have gone through with it had he told me not to. If the media blitz that ensued immediately after this case's victory ever made him regret giving me that blessing, he never told me so.

He was not, however, a pillar of stoicism to the core. One cannot have all one's expectations suddenly removed without it creating some form of emotional turmoil. He couldn't help but wonder what was going to become of me. He worried that the sense of security he felt from having a family was something I would be denied. He knew that even though gay people can and do enter heterosexual marriages and raise families, the majority do not. He could not imagine what a man's life would be like without a family for whom to provide. So after the prom, as my father watched me leaving for California in a whirlwind of publicity, he could only hope and pray that whatever I was to become would not be completely unrecognizable from the person he had expected I would become.

UNDERSTANDING
THE FUTURE

As a kid, I always had hoped I would someday get a chance to go to California. I can't say why, exactly, but looking back on it I cannot disregard the fact that California is about as far away on the map as you can get from Rhode Island and still be in the continental United States. In September of 1980, I got that chance when I made a deal with a Pittsburgh talk show's producers that instead of flying back to Providence, I would take advantage of an equally priced train fare to California.

The train took a few days to cross the country, and during that time I experienced the gradual transformation of both the topography of the country and the landscapes of my perceptions. I was filled with a confident anticipation for my future.

My friend Ed Miskevitch, who had recently moved to California from Rhode Island himself, offered to let me stay with him for three weeks. I had a guaranteed return after that because I had another talk show slated in New York three weeks later. If it seems as though I took these television shows for granted as my free passage back and forth across the United States, I didn't. I always considered them an excellent opportunity to reach young gay people across the country who might feel confused and isolated. I tried not to lose sight of the fact that it had not been so very long since I had been one of them.

I was receiving letters from young and old gay people in response to these talk shows and really felt as if I was tapping into a quiet community. A letter from James Barry of San Gabriel, California, had a special warmth. He was a self-described "gay senior citizen" who offered me the use of his spare room if I was ever in California. "Lots of love and affection," he wrote, "but no sex." This was a gesture on his part to alleviate any fears I might have of becoming entangled in a sexually exploitative situation, and I appreciated that.

During my second day in California, I met Jim Barry and soon realized that the warmth and concern that came through in his letter was consistent with his overall character. Jim turned out to be a sixty-five-year-old man who felt he could offer a gay youth the touch of wisdom and guidance. He guessed I might be an intelligent-enough young man to appreciate the value of this offer. All Jim asked for in return was my susceptibility to influence. He saw this as a great opportunity to share the most valuable thing he had to offer a young gay person, wisdom sparked by genuine empathy. I decided that after the New York talk show, I would return to California and stay with Jim.

Jim did not offer me financial support. Through gentle persuasion, he saw to it that I got myself a job at a local supermarket. At night, he reminded me of the work needed to be done on my book in progress. He called the quiet moments before my writing "our inspirational talks." And they were just that.

During that fall of 1980, I kept in contact with my father in Rhode Island. Upon learning that I was receiving the hospitality and good graces of a sixty-five-year-old man, and the circumstances of how I met him, my father became concerned. The fear that I might be getting by in the world by providing sexual favors for a lecherous sixty-five-year-old was enough to make my dad think he just might have lost me to that world. "That world" is so removed from the mainstream Rhode Islander's perceptions that it is sometimes referred to as the "homosexual world." To my father, whose frame of reference was close enough to that of the mainstream Rhode Islander, it was a world based on sex, where young men forsake critical years of development, only to become lonely old men preying on young men to attain the thing of most importance in this "homosexual world": *sex.*

He had to know! Was this older homosexual programming me with a negative influence, a "homosexual philosophy" as it were? He tossed around the idea of a trip to California to see what was becoming of me. Questions ran through his mind. Would I be willing to share the truth of my new life? Would he be sorry if I did? My father knew that if I was maintaining the standards with which he had raised me, our integral father-son bond would surely be strong enough to overcome any rift caused solely by our different sexual orientations. If, however, being a homosexual meant that I eschewed all semblance of the integrity he was familiar with, I would have to go through life without his acceptance.

It might seem that a father who could cope with his son's homosexuality enough to write a book could accept just about anything. What a great father that would be, right? If so, it's not the kind of father Walter Fricke is. Just because he accepts the fact that I am a homosexual does not mean he gives me carte blanche to do anything. He has said to me, "If you ever commit a murder, don't call me to bail you out of jail." As wrong as it may be to equate the acceptance of murder with the acceptance of homosexuality, the sad fact is that there are scores of fathers who would find it easier to accept a son as a murderer than as a homosexual. Walter Fricke is not one of them.

Partially out of curiosity and partially because he missed his son, he resolved in the spring of 1981 to take a trip to California to visit me. Up to this point, my coming out to my dad had been the most important test of our relationship. After that, I had the feeling that our relationship had survived the ultimate test. Unbeknownst to me, however, my father's trip to California signaled a second, equally volatile time for us. Plans were made: He would come to visit me for two weeks. Jim opened up his home to my father as he had to me, although not in the same words. My father was a little apprehensive, but he accepted Jim's invitation.

It was warm when he arrived in California, especially in contrast to the cold New England climate he had left behind—the environment in which I had grown up. As he drove his rented car from the Los Angeles airport to the house I shared with Jim, his mind tossed back and forth while surrounded by this new Southern California environment: the hot, dry air, the radically different foliage, the overall ambience and attitude. This ambience is perhaps best exemplified by the freeways, which are like constantly flowing rivers into which you cannot jump twice, with their stream of sports cars zooming past his rented car.

He was getting the feeling that maybe my choice to live in this place had, in itself, created distance between us. He realized it was irrational to draw this conclusion from the external stimuli he was receiving, but he also knew that even these superficial elements of the California scenario might represent subtle undertones of my conscious choice to live in a place that would present no reminder of the mores and restriction that living in Rhode Island would demand. My father's apprehensions became so great that his first bit of relief came upon his arrival at the house, when Jim and I answered the door fully clothed. Jim extended a firm handshake, and with direct eye contact said to my dad, "Well, hello, Walter. Come in. What a pleasure it is to meet this fine young man's father." Then once again, my father snapped back to his senses and knew it was illogical to conclude that I had abandoned his code of ethics just because I'd changed my daily scenery.

As my dad entered the house, he was braced for the worst but discovered a well-kept and modest little place. There was no child pornography on the coffee table, no inflatable love dolls lying around, no manacles hanging from the ceiling. And Jim did not appear to be the ungroomed, vulgar human being my dad had feared he might be. Even though first impressions were not exactly inflammatory, he was going to need a lot more reassurance than first impressions could provide.

In any other hands, that first afternoon could have turned out to be intensely discomforting for all parties, marked by numerous pauses and silences as the three of us struggled to find a common ground. We were each from different generations and sensibilities, after all. Jim was in control, however. He had a genuine need for making people feel comfortable and a real flair for doing so. Although I may have been somewhat naïve about the importance of my dad's visit, the gravity of the situation had not escaped Jim. And so for my sake, Jim sincerely put his best foot forward to win my father's acceptance. It was a noble gesture that might have been inconsequential to a less sensitive person, but for Jim this came naturally.

Had my father met Jim on the street, he would not have guessed he was gay, because Jim's manner was in no way stereotypical. (This, in itself, was interpreted by my father as a positive influence on me.) As the afternoon went on, Jim told anecdotes of his thirty years working for the telephone company as a demographics specialist. He had a real interest in my dad's life, too. He lavishly praised my honesty and attributed it to the upbringing I had received. Jim sensed my dad was about ready for a pat on the back. When he was alone with my father, Jim frankly analyzed my strong qualities as well as areas needing improvement, and it was then that my father knew Jim was not just a lot of hot air. After living with me less than a year, Jim seemed to know me as well as, if not better than, my father felt he had come to know me in eighteen. My father intuitively sensed that Jim's interest in me was not lascivious. Plus, Jim made the point of saying he had a strictly platonic relationship with me, and he came across as a man of his word.

My father got the impression that Jim had thought out his words carefully prior to that afternoon, but he did not sense deception in Jim's approach. Even the slightest hint of insincerity would have made Jim seem like an obnoxious phony. What my father saw was a man going out of his way to open up and present himself as someone with values. The effort itself served for my father as confirmation of these values.

When my dad's attention turned toward me, he wondered why I stayed with such an industrious sixty-five-year-old man rather than abandon responsibility, as seemed characteristic of me at times. Now he could not deny that I had consciously made a responsible decision in staying with Jim, and with a firm hand Jim was keeping me right on course. One day during his visit, I asked my dad to shake hands. He complied.

"You did it all wrong, Dad," I scolded. "This is how you're supposed to do it . . . extend your arm and grasp the other person's hand firmly but not overpoweringly, step forward slightly into the handshake, and *never* lose eye contact with the person . . . Jim taught me that!"

My dad was somewhat taken aback to realize he might have been shaking hands improperly for years; but what surprised him even more was my enthusiasm toward something so rooted in common sense. He could see that Jim was teaching me this. It was obvious to my dad that Jim and I had a real sharing bond that subtly transcended the generation gap.

On one of those rare rainy Southern California days, I stayed home while my dad and Jim went to a mall. Jim walked my father around the mall exactly two and a half times, explaining that he was under doctor's orders to walk one mile per day and two and a half times around the mall was precisely one mile. He apologized for dragging my father along, but added that what was good for his own sixty-five-year-old heart could not exactly hurt my dad's younger one. A couple of years previously, Jim had had open-heart surgery, and these walks were part of his therapy. My dad respected Jim's meticulous attention to health. Jim vigorously dismissed the notion of ever lying in a hospital bed helpless and comatose, as his own father had spent years in that condition. The situation had become quite an emotional and financial strain for Jim's family and a great frustration, as the older Mr. Barry never regained consciousness. "That's not my idea of living," Jim said. "I will not allow that to happen to me and I won't put my loved ones through that."

As the days went by, my father became less of a guest and

more of a fixture in Jim's and my daily routine. During a conversation in which I expressed stress about the difficulty I might encounter in college studies, my dad overheard Jim encouraging me to persevere:

"College is most important to your future. Try hard to overcome the hard work with all your will. You have lots when you need it."

My father was impressed that the advice was rooted in an understanding of, and faith in, me. He wished he could talk to me the same way . . . and have me listen. Jim, with his personal understanding of growing up gay, really reached me. I found it easier to give Jim's words credence because they came from a gay person. That was okay with my dad, too, because Jim was not teaching me gay or heterosexual values, but values—period. If, for the time being, Jim was serving as a kind of surrogate father for me, my dad said he could not have handpicked a better heterosexual or homosexual person for the job.

His fears of "outside influences" were turning into prayers of thanks for the outside influence I was receiving. He saw me getting the guidance he wished he could give me but knew that he couldn't. Firstly, I lived three thousand miles away. Besides that, though, there were things that he could not teach me because he himself also was learning them from Jim.

When it came time for him to leave California, his feelings were radically different from the anxiety he had felt upon arrival. He had discovered that his fears of my corruption were unfounded. Our relationship had passed another important crossroads and he was relieved. My basic values were intact.

My father learned more on that vacation than just my status in the world, however. Against all expectations, he encountered a sixty-five-year-old homosexual whom he could whole-heartedly respect. Jim showed my father that the "homosexual world" does not have to be devoid of love. And as he watched me eagerly accepting Jim's leadership, he knew that I wanted to make the best of myself. Any fears he had of a lonely old age for me diminished on that vacation, because if I could maintain the integrity and quality of life Jim lived, he knew that I would be loved.

Even though my father went home and I eventually moved out on my own, we both made sure to keep closely in touch with Jim. In the ensuing years that we knew Jim, we both came to learn that one can love a nonrelative just as sincerely as one can love one's own bloodline. No matter what age, sex, color, class, and so on, a person with such qualities as honesty, integrity, and a legitimate concern for others will find themselves loved. Jim Barry possessed all of these qual-ities.

Two and a half years later when Jim was at dinner with his friend Byron one night, he told Byron to call him the next day. Jim said that if Byron got no answer, it would mean he was dead. The next day at twelve noon, Jim's phone rang but no one answered. Even at the end, Jim was as methodical and in control of his death as he was of his life.

Byron's first calls to me went unanswered also, because as fate would have it, that fall of 1983, I was at school working my way through some tough college courses. Jim would have been proud.

Later that day when I eventually did find out about Jim's death, I called my father with the bad news. We cried to-gether. Jim's death represented the loss of a very special mem-ber of our family.

Perhaps the healthiest attitude is the one that recognizes the whole human race as one big family. As idealistic as this may sound, in the global twentieth century it should not be so impossible for people to extend the boundaries of tribal mentality. Neighbors nowadays include everyone from a literal next-door neighbor, who may be an up-and-coming Yuppie, to a starving person living halfway around the world in Ethiopia—or maybe even the sixty-five-year-old homosexual living in your own town.

CONFLICT

I n the summer of 1984, my father was sitting in a restaurant with a homosexual he loved, namely me. A few months earlier, we had decided it might be a neat idea to write a book together. It was really that spontaneous. He was proud of me for already having one published book, and when I told him there had never been a book written by a heterosexual father and a gay son, he said we should do it. So at the time, I had returned to the East Coast to take a one-week vacation with him in Provincetown, Massachusetts, to get started on gathering our insights for this prospective book.

In winter, Provincetown is a quaint fishing village with a small population of mostly Portuguese families, but in the summertime, its population explodes with thousands upon thousands of gay people. Many Provincetown cafés, bars, and small businesses stay closed during the barren winter months and reopen to accommodate this summer population. We

were sitting in a restaurant that thrives on the summer's pre-
dominantly gay clientele.

We looked out the restaurant window and saw many people
in wild costumes on Commercial Street, Provincetown's main
drag. People in wild costumes were not really that unusual
in Provincetown, but the high concentration of them that
evening suggested to us that a special celebration was taking
place. Our waitress, who _____ _____ _____
West, confirmed _____ _____ festi_____ _____
town Mardi Gras. _____ suspicio_____ _____ _____
as well as on the street.

While taking our order, the waitress reeled out a _____
of off-color remarks in true Mae West fashion. At first, none
of these seemed targeted directly at us. Then when my dad
lightly objected to a particularly expensive appetizer I or-
dered, Mae West was launched.

To him: "Whassa mattuh, can't affawd 'im?"

To me: "You better tell the old man he's gotta do right
by ya or ya ain't gonna do 'im at all. Ooh, ooh."

I winced. My father conceded on the appetizer, swept up
in the ebullient spirit of it all. While waiting for the appetizer
to arrive, however, something about what Mae West had said
was eating at him.

"Why did she talk that way? Doesn't she realize I'm your
father?" he wondered.

"She thinks you're my dad all right, my sugar daddy."

Now *he* winced.

"Naw, c'mon, Aaron. That's not even funny."

"Funny or not, trust me on this one, Dad." I was just as
embarrassed as my father, but I wondered whether he was
presenting a pseudonaïveté about this—it seemed so obvious.
I already had seen us in that psychological storefront window

My father with his father in a photo taken sometime in the late Twenties.

that one's mind glances at occasionally to check out how one appears to others. I knew the waitress assumed we were lovers.

"You're wrong, Aaron. I'll ask her." Evidently, it was not so obvious to my dad. "I just want to know. . . . You'll see, Aaron, that's not what she thinks."

"Okay. Okay, Dad. I agree, that's not what she thinks. Just drop it, *please.*" I was desperate to avoid the embarrassment lurking in this situation. The subject was not brought up again during dinner and I was relieved.

Curiosity, however, got the better of my dad, because when I returned from the bathroom after dinner, he had a numb look of shock on his face when he said, "Well, much as I hate to admit it, you were right. I told her I am your father."

"And what did she say?"

"She said, 'Sure, sure, anything you say, big boy.' "

"Ohmigod! Embarrassment!" His numb look of shock became infectious.

I knew from the beginning what the waitress really thought. What I didn't know was how my dad would react to this. For the first time in his life, he had become acutely aware of the integral link between his sexuality and his persona. He didn't like being identified as a homosexual. Worst of all, he was assumed to be gay simply because he was seen with me. Assuming a person is gay in this place is not a slur, but a way of embracing an individual, of letting a person know that being gay just made you a member of the group. My dad had always been presumed to be heterosexual by a world that looks that way upon people who blend in. Provincetown in summer is really not a part of that world; those who stand out blend in, those who blend in stand out. Assuming that my dad was gay was just this society's way of extending itself to him. Anywhere else, he might have complained to the management if a waitress assumed he was gay. But Provincetown in summer is not anywhere else.

It's true, we had been visiting Provincetown together since I was a little boy, but things had changed since then. I had changed, he had changed, we had changed. In that interim, I had grown up gay, come out to my father, sued my high school and won the legal right to attend my senior prom with a male date, and even had written a book about all of it. Way back when I was a little boy, my dad never could have imagined sitting in one of the P-town restaurants being taken for my lover. But here we were.

At twenty-two years old, and four years since I had left home, I was living my life in places like this. That is not to say I was spending my life vacationing in gay resorts, but the atmosphere in my new surroundings was, in my father's eloquent wording, "gay." It's true that much of the input in my life had a homosexual orientation. The people I associated with were homosexuals; the periodicals I read were geared toward the gay community; even much of the literature I read had some kind of gay slant.

My attitude in my dealings with my dad was becoming undeniably precocious. My enthusiasm was energized by the hope that he might be fascinated by some of my unique new perceptions of the world. I was enthralled by the new people, their new vocabulary, the new political ideals that I had encountered in the four years since leaving Rhode Island, and I was bound and determined to regurgitate every last morsel of this newly digested ideology. His indifference toward these ideas only irked me and egged me on.

While lounging on a Provincetown beach, a conversation took place that was typical of the way our communications were changing, turning toward the antagonistic.

"Whoo-ee! What a mouse!" He cooed at an attractive woman walking by.

I was caught off guard and quickly looked in the direction of my father's glance, then slowly and resentfully turned back to him and rolled my eyes.

He continued to make these comments every so often. He was lightly teasing me but he was doing a little exploring, too. He really had never gotten to know a homosexual as closely as he knew me. On a purely clinical level, he was surprised that any male could be so oblivious to the gorgeous females passing by. On a more personal level, he hoped to stir some call of the wild in me by pointing out attractive women.

"Would ya get a load a' that, Aaron. . . . What a looker!"

I knew my dad was just doing what dads do with their sons, but I found this prodding totally inappropriate under the circumstances. This might be a ritual that encourages male bonding between heterosexual fathers and sons, but for us, this situation was a sign of impending conflict.

"Mm-mm, that's *some* chicken." He paused, got me to look him square in the eye, and with an incredulous expression on his face said, "Now, you can't tell me that girl doesn't do anything for you."

That was it! I had suffered the last blow to my sensibilities. I verbally lunged at him.

"First of all, Dad, these so called 'girls' you are leering at are not girls at all. When they're over eighteen, they're referred to as 'women.' Calling a woman a girl reeks of the disrespect that people use to dismiss women!"

This only confused my father.

"What's the big deal? All I did was point out a few girls."

"*Ugh!* . . . And second of all, these women you are cruising are lesbians. You are pointing out lesbian women to a gay man. Does the irony of this strike you as at all poignant?"

My frustration was overwhelming me. My dad was not about to give in.

"Knock it off! I'm not *croo*-sing lesbians. . . . I'm just doing a little birdwatchin'."

"That attitude is Neanderthal, Dad. Can't you crawl out of that primordial-soup mentality?"

A game of antagonistic Ping-Pong had begun between us.

"Oh, Aaron, stop acting so gay."

"*What the hell is that supposed to mean?* I *am* gay, Dad. Get that through your thick skull."

A fight had broken out.

"When you act that way, people won't want anything to do with you. I'm your father and I don't even want to be seen with you when you're acting that way."

No holds barred.

"Do you hear what you're saying, Dad? Don't you realize that is exactly the kind of attitude that all my life I have struggled to . . ."

And so it went back and forth, and the confrontational undertones did not stop that day or on that Provincetown vacation. The provocation for these wranglings changed, but as time passed, increasing hostility crept into all of our interactions. The unfortunate irony in this was that these confrontations grew from our initial efforts to reach out to each other. The problem was that our sensibilities had evolved in such radically different directions that they actually offended each other. There was no rift in our substratum principles, but a crack as prominent as the San Andreas Fault presented itself between our more surface ideals—in essence, our politics. This contrast would prove to be our undoing. My father heard my thoughts steeped in subversive rhetoric. I considered his opinions to be fascistic. And our ingrained predispositions toward bullheadedness did not exactly help matters.

My father's totally unyielding way of responding to my viewpoints led me to taunt him with a crash course in alternative lifestyles. I privately howled at the way his facial expression would plummet when I used terms such as *bondage and discipline* and *fat fems*. These words had been desensitized for me before I had even graduated from high school. Now, a few years into my twenties, I could recall only vicariously the sting those words once had by watching my dad's face contort as they were spoken. For me, it was a hoot. I was busting my dad's balls. He was not quite so amused.

He didn't realize that my actions were a cry for acknowledgment. I didn't realize that since he had acknowledged and formed strong negative opinions of liberal schools of thought long before, his self-imposed detachment was really a gesture of diplomacy and respect.

Any airs of diplomacy between us were to be short-lived, however. Much of what my father felt most shocked by was my brutal frankness. He couldn't figure out whether I was broadening my horizons or sailing to the point of no return. He wondered whether I was out of the closet or out of the ballpark. His blood boiled, for instance, when he asked me in a phone conversation what I had done during the week and I replied, "I got rejected by some guy at the baths." In this instance, I was being a bit more brutal than frank. Still, he knew it was time to offer me a lesson in what ball-busting is all about.

I was already into work on this book in early 1985 when I asked him to put pen to paper with some thoughts. I received this tract in return.

Walter looks at gays in general

Gays are, for the most part, irresponsible people who don't pay bills. Most of them have no loyalty to principles or moral values. Certainly not long term. Nothing challenges them, except their next partner. They appear to be happy on the surface, but sad with life in general. They drift into the job they hold rather than pursue it with diligence. They are unimpressed by ordinary persons. . . . Perhaps that is why so many of them go into the performing arts.

Then he addressed "The fears the ordinary man has of homosexuals," saying, "To think of an erect penis up there is sickening."

His letter was accompanied by an article on Acquired Immune Deficiency Syndrome, with the following comment penciled at the top: "I realize that sending you this article is kind of like sending a smoker information on lung cancer."

My palm hit my forehead with a thunderous clap as I read the letter. I responded to him with an article on male menopause.

Neither one of us knew exactly how our relationship had become so antagonistic, but this was far from over. Under the ruse of writing this book, we kept heckling each other. It was as if our father/son relationship was foundering and the book became the one life preserver to fight over. Common sense should have told both of us that the only course of survival would be to turn away and swim for solid ground; but the struggle went on.

As his attitudes became more negative, the more positively I portrayed them in my writing. It was a reflexive defense mechanism. I wanted to write a truthful book with a message of affirmation and hope, and I refused to accept the reality of my deteriorating relationship with my dad. So I resorted to cheating reality by creating one of my own. Take, for example, this passage I originally slipped into one of my father's chapters.

> Opening his mind to understand and accept Aaron as a homosexual was a slow and painful struggle for Walter. But Walter could not imagine a harsher anguish than losing his son because of closed-minded obstinance. Walter was now disgusted with a world that could bring itself to deny homosexuals equal rights. [The book was originally written in the third person.]

I created a flag-waving, militant, activist parent as a blatant way of dismissing the real parent I had. Upon reading this, he figured that if I was going to create a version of a father and tailor it to my own likes and dislikes, then it was only fair that he get the chance to take the artistic license and do a little recreating of the son he got stuck with. The conflicts of our relationship and the conflicts of collaborating on this book were becoming inextricably intertwined, tripping each other up, and bringing both the relationship and the book ever so much closer to a dead end.

Meanwhile, I was undergoing a special kind of experience on my own. I often was invited to speak to gay people at colleges, community centers, and various gay groups across the United States and even one in Central America. I had been given the incredible opportunity to observe different people in different places, even in different cultures. And each of these groups of people embraced me as one of their own. I was receiving a wondrous and enlightening exposure to the world that I never in my wildest dreams could have imagined would be the fruit of my labors on *Reflections of a Lobster*. I would drop my dad a postcard from each of the places I visited. He was invariably unimpressed.

He simply couldn't see anything being accomplished. His sensibilities lay in a world in which a man's course for success was a well-charted one. When he thought *success*, he thought *college diploma*. I was still studying nutrition in college but was clearly more impressed by what I was learning outside of the textbooks. I had not forgotten what my dad taught me about the importance of having knowledge, but I was coming to appreciate the discipline college gave me to interpret and assimilate a variety of information more than the knowledge I was accumulating studying dietetics. My father was not only frustrated by my artistic sensibility but it also frightened him a little bit.

He saw that aside from everything else, I had no business

sense. I had made money from my first book, but to me money has always been a kind of peripheral privilege, in no way related to the reason for working and in no way comparable to the spiritual compensations of life. My father knew that anyone, artist or not, would be eaten alive by the modern workday world if they didn't have some awareness of how to use their talents to make money. My steadfast obliviousness to this led my father to fear for my financial future.

When Jim Barry died, he bequeathed me a substantial amount of money in his will. In a fit of artistic expression, I took a lot of the money and invested it in a variety of film equipment. Then I set about spending a lot more of it on the budget for my film, *Dan White: Justice at Last*. And thanks to the incomparably brilliant and insightful playwright Robert Patrick, *Dan White* was given a theatrical venue at the Fifth Estate Theater in Hollywood. Because I labeled the film "trash," I refused to charge any more than two dollars' admission (and that only after considerable persuasion from Mr. Patrick), so whatever profit potential the film might have had was doomed. Even after losing my ass, I felt the entire experience a good one for having given me the opportunity to create something.

But this bravado was a glamorous rationalization on my part and my father knew it. He could see me developing a somewhat overly romanticized idea of who I was and what my place in the world was. Jim's firm hand and conservative approach were missing from my life. So my dad thought it might be in my best interest if he made an attempt to douse my eternal flame.

COMBAT

By mid-1986, when he hadn't received any new book material in months, my father gave me a call. A little bit into the conversation, he clobbered me.

"My own pleasure comes from seeing others grow. When are you going to reward me with this pleasure?"

I was caught off guard.

"What's up your ass, Dad?"

"I'm just saying your performance rep has not been all it should be for twenty-four years old. I hope you can face that one."

I regained my composure.

"Well, your performance rep as a father leaves something to be desired, too."

"I am your father and I love you a lot more than these friends of yours who tell you you're God's gift to the homosexual world."

"Don't tell me how much my friends love me. When Bob and I broke up, Jon jumped on a plane, came out here, and just held my hand for a week because he knew what I was going through. Did you even try to understand?"

"Screw him!"

"And my friend Bif Blintz's father just bought Bif a new house. Do you know how that makes me feel when all I get from you is put-downs?"

"Buying you a house isn't going to show you that I love you, Aaron."

"It wouldn't hurt."

By now, every defense had gone up between us and all our interactions were becoming man-to-man combat, with both of us trying to gain a little ground on the other.

"I'm twenty-four years old, I've written a book, I've been on 'Donahue' *twice*. What more do you want?"

"I told you I would just like to see some sign that you're a mature adult."

"You couldn't see it if it hit you on the head, Dad. I've got a published book registered in the Library of Congress. Do you realize that at age twenty-four, I have achieved immortality? That is something you may never have, because with every conversation this book between you and me is becoming more and more hopeless."

Hopeless was right.

"No, Aaron. The only immortality lies in one's children."

"Okay, so I'm an author and I'm your son . . . now there's family immortality. So what's your point?"

People have said I have an annoying gift for turning an argument around by reducing it to the fragments of whatever ideas I believe at a given time. My father felt this was one of those instances and he was flabbergasted with disbelief. He asked himself, Does my son actually expect to achieve immortality through these books for homosexuals?

By this point, there was no way to tell for sure. Every single moment of our interactions had become a defensive reaction to some previous interaction. I was reacting to what I perceived as my father's disrespect toward my right and ability to make my own decision on how to live my life.

Nevertheless, my claim to immortality hit him especially hard because there will be no more Frickes in our family line. I happen to be the last of this Fricke family (for which there is a family coat of arms sitting in my dad's uncle's attic). My father is the last, but he has two children: Cheryl, who has had children, but they bear a different surname, and me. And here I was telling my father I was going to honor and perpetuate the family name by writing books for homosexuals. It seemed to my dad that I had missed the whole point of life.

He was under the mistaken impression that his words meant little to me; but on the contrary, his words had great impact. I just didn't understand that he was being hard on me for my own good. No matter, because by this point, my dad was coming to the conclusion that whatever I learned in life was obviously going to have to be learned on my own. He was heartbroken that his attempts to help me were becoming undeniably futile, but he could not continue the psychological drain of wondering whether or not I had assimilated the discipline it takes to make it in a coldhearted world. Whatever I learned, I would obstinately insist on learning for myself. So be it—he figured he had said all he could say.

What he had said convinced me that work on this book should be abandoned. I decided to stop writing to him, as well. He was not alarmed when he did not hear from me for a couple of months. In fact, he was somewhat relieved, because he did not have to field my frequent requests for money. He believed with the sincerest form of love that sending me money at that point would only destroy me. He had given all that he felt he owed me, not the least of which was a college education. We both had come to the point where we could enjoy a temporary respite from each other.

Around Christmas of 1986, however, he became a little concerned when he called me and received a disconnect recording. He had no other phone number to contact me, so he sent me a check for one hundred dollars. The way he figured it, this was a foolproof way of finding out whether or not I was alive, since as long as I lived and breathed, nothing short of a comatose state would prevent me from accepting free money.

I received the check, all right, but knew full well the backhanded sentiment behind it. I could have used the money at the time, but my dignity was not for sale, so I tossed the check. I was adapting to life on my own but was still trapped in this game of cat and mouse with him. So I followed suit by not responding to him in any way. If he was worried, I was determined to make him sweat.

He was not, however, doing that much sweating. He was concerned but somehow sensed I was surviving. In the meantime, his life was moving on, too, and he was not having an especially difficult time adapting to life without me around.

In reality, we were not out of each other's lives at all. Because even though these provoking little gestures of antagonism were all that was left to our relationship, they were real forms of an abstract kind of expression going on between us. We were growing further apart because of all this psychological maneuvering, but it was also sadly true that this argumentative interaction had become the factor that was keeping us together. It had become the one familiar form of adult communication to which we had become accustomed. The relationship had sunk pretty low, but our lives were not so separate and isolated as to be devoid of all contact—not yet, at least.

After six months of not hearing from me, he made a final effort—with this letter—to reach me in January of 1987:

Aaron,

If your failure to contact me was designed to make me worry about you, then I grant that you have succeeded.

I remember so clearly the day you fell ass over teakettle down the steps at Hunter Pharmacy. And the day I fell and lost my balance and you said, "I'll help you find it, Daddy." What happened to the kid who could play the piano so well; the kid who took those scholastic tests and came in the 91st percentile in the USA; the kid who made best camper two years in a row at Beach Pond Camp? What happened to that kid?

Last night I was listening to a tape I made many years ago while your mother and I were arguing. I felt terrible for the little boy I heard in the background (you) and I just wished there was a way to turn back the clock and change your life. You really were a good kid. And I often wondered if I had left your mother, would I have been better off. But I was sure then and am sure now that *you* would have been worse off. Remember, I didn't have the benefit of a father's guidance [his father died when he was ten] and perhaps that's why I've always been so concerned about you. But that's all in the past now.

I have come to the realization that I am a nice guy and that even though there is much I could share with my children and grandchildren, the opportunity may never present itself. So my only choice is to move on to others who appreciate me.

I am here for you always.

I will continue to pray for you.

God bless you,
Dad

Despite the warm comment "I am here for you always," all I could hear was, "You really *were* a good kid. . . . What happened?" I interpreted his letter as a fond farewell, a haughty kiss-off. I felt awful. In all my unyielding avoidance of my father during the previous months, I never seriously thought he would give up the pursuit. Even though the words were not literally spelled out in the letter, I felt the general tone of it confirmed that my father had psychologically prepared himself to write me off.

I was disillusioned. I started blaming myself for letting the situation get so out of hand. Up until then, I had never appreciated the high stakes involved in the challenges I entered into with my dad. Now I was shaken by the possibility of having lost him. This was exactly how he hoped I might react to the letter.

This feeling of total exhaustion did not last. All too quickly, I had a whole new set of defenses. Rather than accept that he wrote the letter to teach me the importance of a parent/

child relationship, I began to rationalize that he had written it with anything but good intentions.

I convinced myself that he did not mean what he had said in the letter, that it was all just his clever way of riling me up. That wasn't an astute enough rationalization, however, since I could not help but be riled and that meant admitting I had succumbed to my father's manipulation. So I confronted my worst fear: that he really *didn't* give a shit anymore. If that was so, why? Then suddenly I recalled that a scandalous reason had prompted a similar kind of parental rejection on "All My Children" once. I called my mother to ask her a serious question.

"Um . . . Mom, this is going to sound weird . . . but Dad has been really cold toward me lately and . . . well . . . I've always taken for granted that he *is* my father but . . . um . . . this isn't easy . . . is there anything I don't know?"

"*What?*" She was not expecting that.

"Now please don't take offense, Mom. I just want to know. He doesn't treat me like my father anymore. So I just want to know, is there any possibility that—"

"No, Aaron." My mom said this with gentle reassurance, as she could sense the pain in my voice for having to ask.

"You're sure, Mom? Because if so, you can tell me. I'm not even sure I'm ever going to talk to him again."

"I promise you, Aaron, Walter Fricke is your father. If there were even the faintest possibility otherwise, I would tell you."

Her motherly instincts took over.

"What is going on? Did *he* plant this in your mind?"

"No, no, no. It's just that this letter he sent me gave me the feeling that he doesn't care about me anymore."

"He's good at that. . . . You *do* realize he's in prison right now, don't you?"

"*What?*" I was not expecting *that*.

"Oh, I thought you'd know by now. He owed me and my lawyers close to one hundred thousand dollars and refused to sign over a Merrill Lynch Keough plan to pay them off. So last week the divorce-court judge said, 'You either sign that piece of paper, Mr. Fricke, or you'll go to jail today.' Your father still wouldn't sign it, so they took him away."

I could not believe what I was hearing. I could hardly accept that my father could be so foolish as to defy a judge's orders. It was hard for me to comprehend why he was acting like a child and letting his emotions get in the way of an inflexible legal process. I struggled to understand why he wouldn't just sign the damned paper. I knew my father wasn't an imbecile and assumed he had to realize that there are proper ways to see that justice is served. It seemed to me that his defiance of the judge's ruling flew in the face of justice. I could not respect what my father was doing, nor could I bring myself to laugh at him. Instead, I felt an overwhelming sense of disgrace. My shame did not arise from the simple fact that my father was in jail but from what I thought was a senseless reason for him willingly to go to jail. I could respect someone for standing up for a lot of things but could not find it in my heart to respect the only thing I believed he was really standing up for: *money.*

After considerable inquiry and thought was given to the matter, my interpretation of the whole scenario was this: When the judge told him to sign the piece of paper or go to jail, my father was given the formidable task of choosing to retain only one of two monumental concepts, his money or his freedom. By refusing to sign the document, I felt he had chosen money over freedom. He truly became a tragic figure in my eyes. I was dumbstruck that this was the same person who had continuously told me that *my* priorities were screwed up.

Parents so often try, with their own lives, to set a good example for their kids to follow. It sometimes happens, however, that these are the very examples from which their kids glean how *not* to act. This stand of my father's taught me some valuable lessons, but assuredly nothing he intended. His grandstanding evoked some strong anticapitalistic sentiments in me.

It occurred to me that because of my father's programming as a child during the Depression years, everything good about his life, and every human quality that made his life good, had an irreversible association with having money. I was sure that even his self-respect had become so closely equated with money that he could not imagine that there could be dignity without collateral. My father's willingness to sacrifice his freedom before parting with his money served as symbolic proof to me that there existed tragic drawbacks to his capitalistic approach to life.

I was hardly on a crusade against capitalism, though. I was just reacting with disgust toward the disgrace I felt my father caused. I almost privately wished my mother had said that he was not my father. Since he was in jail, I had no chance to share any of this with him, but in a final gesture of disrespect, the equivalent of spitting in his face, I contacted his girlfriend and, after many months of not hearing from me at all, I got her to ask him to send me a check from jail.

Of course, he was aghast at this request. As he sat in his jail cell, dwelling, as men in jail sometimes tend to do, on his life's suffering, he grew more than just a little disappointed in his son. He believed I had changed from a hardworking, thoughtful, likable kid into an inconsiderate, unmanageable, and insensitive man. This was exactly how I hoped he might react.

That was it, the end. Our father/son relationship, which had allowed us to overcome the first major conflict because of our different sexual orientations and survived long enough for us to see that our fundamental values did not clash, was now torn to shreds by what was essentially our individual tenacity about our radically different approaches to life.

OUR SEPARATE WAYS

There would be no more struggling over this book as there would be no more struggling over the relationship. In late January of 1987, our lives became totally separate and isolated. He briefly entertained the idea of starting over by having another son, and I buried the abandoned work on this book in a bottom drawer, hiding it as the only physical reminder that my father ever existed.

He was released from jail after four months when my mother's lawyers found a way to break open his Merrill Lynch account without his signature. Amazingly, he emerged from jail with a renewed belief in himself. He was confident he could make it in life without his former wife or the kid who had turned on him. He turned to his girlfriend, who had visited him every day during his imprisonment, with a restored faith in the concept of love. This woman was a fifty-year-old divorceé who provided him with a ready-made family of loving children and grandchildren. These were the people who comforted him while I shunned him. The new people enveloped him and helped him erase the memories of turmoil in his past. He did not allow himself to forget or stop loving me; he was just going to switch his focus to people around him who appreciated him as a nice guy. After sixty years of his life, he felt that he had finally attained a sense of equanimity.

My life was not to proceed quite as smoothly during the next two years. I turned to my California friends and they reaffirmed for me that I had an unworthy father. This provided me with the sort of energy I thought I needed in order to carry on.

I spent much time at the house Bif Blintz's father bought. Bif and I had become close friends a couple of years earlier when he found out he had been exposed to the HIV virus that causes AIDS. He told me that he had formerly been a prostitute in Los Angeles and he assumed that was where he had contracted the virus. I had helped Bif through some psychologically tough times back then, and at this point Bif was helping me out through my hard times by letting me stay at the house.

I thought I was developing some pretty close alliances with the people who came and went from Bif's house. Most of them were hustlers, and even though I wasn't, they were all friendly enough to me. I came to feel as though I even could trust them. Then a few months later, I noticed a lot of unauthorized activity on my bank machine card. Upon checking my bank statement, I discovered that the little money I had saved was now nearly gone. Someone at Bif's house had learned my secret code and had gained access to my account, depleting my money.

I felt used. I could not point an accusing finger at any individual, but someone in the house obviously had been stealing my money. Months after rejecting my father, I had imagined myself by this point to have established a trusting relationship with these new people in my life. Perhaps I had a special need to feel this trust *because* of my loss of faith in my dad. Someone who had been listening to me lament my sad story about my father and *his* love of money was all the time thinking of ways to get at *my* money. I was apparently not as strongly anticapitalistic about my own money as I was about my father's. I interpreted this incident as a lesson that no matter how strongly I felt about his actions, I had to stop glorifying my father's shame.

Because of a technicality, the bank reimbursed all of the money I lost except for fifty dollars. I used this money to move out of Bif's and get my own apartment. I eventually found out who had been responsible and was relieved that it was not Bif. He had all the money he wanted from his father. We remained friends.

On Bif's advice, I took a job as clerk at the local adult bookstore/peep-show establishment. My job duties included handing out quarters for the X-rated video booths and selling numerous polyurethane "novelty items." Within a couple of months after taking this job, I was at work when one of Southern California's notorious earthquakes struck, sending various "back-door kits," "autosucks" and "mini-dongs" crashing down onto my head. By this point, I believed I had lost all love for my father; my money had been stolen by people I trusted; and now, faced with the threat of imposing sex devices hurling toward me, I was at a loss to figure out what it all meant. One thing was for sure, it wasn't going to take much more to get me to stop trying.

It should be noted at this point that my best friend, Jon Carr, remained the one constant throughout all of this. Even though Jon was three thousand miles away in New York City, it can safely be said that without his spiritual guidance, I would not have made it through. That, however, is another book.

My friendship with Bif, although much more immediate in physical proximity, was about to be proved light-years away in terms of moral values. Bif began hustling in front of the adult bookstore. I was in shock and felt compelled to confront him about this.

"Bif, what are you doing?"

"What does it look like I'm doing? I'm engaging in a little free enterprise, girlfriend."

"But Bif, sex *should* be a free enterprise. Why are you doing this? I thought your father gave you all the money you needed."

"He does, girl. But I figure it's not fair to everyone else to be his whore exclusively."

"That's not even funny, Bif."

"Oh, girl. I like doing this. I thought you knew that."

Evidently, Bif had just stopped hustling to give himself time to psychologically recuperate after finding out he was HIV-positive, in much the same way I had stopped writing to have time to psychologically recuperate from falling out with my father.

"But what would your father think if he knew you were doing this, Bif?"

"Girl, my father traffics drugs to get his money in the first place. If I get caught, I just call him to bail me out. He couldn't give a shit less what I do."

"*I* give a shit, Bif. Knowing that you're HIV-positive, I think it's my duty as your friend to tell you I can't respect you for doing this."

"Oh, fuck off, girl."

Bif took great offense at what I had said and resolved to

get back at me for having said it. Since I *had* thought of Bif as a close friend, he came to know some of the smaller details of my life. For instance, Bif was aware that I was trying to save enough money to pay off a warrant that had been issued when I failed to appear in court for a minor traffic violation. So, to spite me for having been so arrogant as to suggest he did not belong hustling, Bif delivered the address of my place of employment to the police.

I was behind the counter when the cops came in. My arrest was handled matter-of-factly. I was not treated like a serious criminal. The police knew of the reputation of the person who had turned me in. They allowed me to continue working for another half-hour until a relief could get in. It was an extremely humiliating half-hour standing behind that counter guarded by two policemen while Bif's hustler friends came into the store smirking at me. However, I did not break down and cry until I was in the squad car on the way to jail. Then I cried, wondering how it ever had happened that I had become so lost in this mire.

In the past, I had made the conscious decision never to lose faith in people. I thought that if the choice was between being paranoid and suspicious of people in order never to be hurt and having a basic faith in people no matter how vulnerable it made me, the choice had to be faith. I never wanted to become one of those people who, in choosing the security of the first option, sacrifice such a large chunk of their own humanity. Although now, slowly but surely, it was becoming clear to me that my own intense need to have faith in people had overshadowed the reality of the people in whom I had placed this faith. I was beginning to lose faith in my own faith. I was confused. I was to have the next fourteen days in jail to sort all of this out in my mind, however.

In my jail cell, there was a small window out of which I

could see. There wasn't that much to see, mostly just the tops of trees, but I found myself appreciating this view more than I ever had appreciated a view. During my first days in jail, I looked out the window and felt my mind roam over the tops of the trees out toward the horizon. Then one evening as I watched a sunset, I found myself appreciating the moment so intensely that tears began welling up in my eyes. I was not crying because I wanted to be outside feeling this sunlight on my face, but for all the time I *had* felt sunlight on my face and not appreciated it. I was crying because I was suddenly realizing that being able to appreciate life is what freedom really is, and that the more I appreciated, the more free I was. I was learning that truth can lie in the beauty of a moment.

Then I found myself not wanting to let that moment go. I knew that if the moment did not go, though, my jail stay would not progress; it would stay forever at three days. I realized that life has to be a series of moments in succession or it is not life. There is no point to hanging on; just appreciate a moment and let it go. I accepted that I must have faith that every sunset will be followed by an even better dawn. And as my father had taught me that every lie will lead to another, even bigger lie, I was about to learn on my own that every truth will be followed by another, even greater truth.

As it so happened, this period of time was around Christmas 1987. On Christmas Eve, there was a chapel call. I thought about going, but when a number of men got up to go, I decided to stay, feeling the religious experience might be diminished by the group. When the group returned, they had some Christmas decorations that they had swiped from the chapel. There wasn't much, just one yellow Christmas ball and a four-inch snap of evergreen that one guy referred to as "our tree." At that point, I saw a middle-aged guy jump up, grab the snap, and pull it to his nose for a deep whiff. For one brief moment, I could see that the man's eyes had been transposed; his soul had been liberated to sometime in the past, perhaps to relive one glorious moment of a wondrous boyhood. In looking at this man, I found myself transported as well to a time in my life when things were a lot simpler than they had come to be.

I was remembering that some of the simplest, least complicated times of my life had been spent with my father. I could now see that no matter what new ways I would come up with to look at life, there were certain permanent truths in my life that my father had had a fundamental role in determining. It was during my time in jail, under the most dire of circumstances, that I was turning back to these truths and finding comfort. Here in this male-dominated institution, I was beginning to understand what my father meant by "the discipline it takes to make it in a coldhearted world."

By the time I was released from jail three days after Christmas, I had regained faith in my own faith. It was as if in going to jail I had to go off and change a little bit before I could come back to appreciate what I always had known. I could see clearly that I had allowed the wrong people in my life to take on more importance than my own father. I felt guilty about having done this. I could not help but wonder whether all my harsh feelings toward him might have resulted from some adolescent need I had *to* lose faith in him. I saw the enormous possibility that the rift with my father could have been a curious stage in a growth process that allowed me the space to go off and learn on my own what my father had been trying to teach me all along. Of course, what he had been trying to teach me all along was not that I should have faith in him but that I should have faith in myself and in God.

RESOLUTION

I decided that I would try to sort out and unravel the mistakes I had made in dealing with my father. I knew that this was not the sort of psychological undertaking that would occur overnight, but I was sure that if I could come to understand *why* I had feelings of resentment toward him, I could release them. After months of wading through all the complicated emotions involved, I condensed it to this: The overwhelming sense of disgrace I had felt toward my father was just an easy excuse to write him out of my life. I saw that I had resented him for what I deemed his stubborn behavior in going to jail. With my new perspective, however, I wondered whether going to jail could, in itself, represent my father's freedom of political expression, just as going to the prom had represented mine. He had granted me respect then, even though he didn't really share my cause, but I would not allow him the same privilege to follow through on his own principles. I knew that it was really my father's inner resolve that I resented and I knew I had not been fair to him, or myself. I had inadvertently condemned him for the very character that I had, by nature or nurture, inherited from him. In disrespecting my father, I might as well have been disrespecting myself. My final conclusion was that hating your parents for what they made you is just another way of hating yourself for what you've become.

There is something about not accepting your parents that is akin to not accepting yourself. I was beginning to realize that I had somehow allowed my negative feelings toward my father to overthrow my love of everything else. I pulled the discarded work on this book out of my bottom drawer. I saw in the black and white of those typewritten pages my creation of a different father than the one I had. There was no ambivalence in this father's acceptance. This father made sweeping pronouncements of approval. This father was "untainted by the misguided fears that heterosexual society inflicts upon its members." For the first time, however, I could see that as progressive and politically correct as that fabricated patriarch was, he just could not compare to the symmetry of the total human being that my father really is.

I couldn't help but question whether maybe it was this book that had undermined the entire relationship in the first place. I realized that I had become so bent on creating the object that I lost track of and became dissatisfied with the subject. I could see how this blasé attitude toward the strength of reality led me to lose faith in myself as a writer, and as a person. From there, scapegoating my father for the collapse of this entire project was just a short baby step away.

If it was my writing that had gotten me into that mess, I knew it was going to have to be my writing that got me out of it. This project had come to represent my entire relationship with my father. It was more than just coincidence that both had expired simultaneously. I wanted to contact him but sensed I was not quite ready. My heart told me to contact my father immediately, but my pride was holding me back. To let go of that pride, I once again turned to my writing. In the late summer of 1988, I almost felt possessed as I wrote the following personal letter to myself in response to this predicament:

I really need to touch base with some aspects of my life. My life is at a crucial crossroad. I am intelligent and capable of continued growth. I can recognize the subtle choices life presents me. What I have here is a choice. I have the opportunity to grow with this choice. Point blankly, either I forget my father ever existed or I find a way to appreciate him. The choice is now. There can be no more delay, I sense. And what choice is there really? What kind of conscience would I live with if I was to continue discrediting my father's significance in my life?

Getting back on course is not some vague concept of overwhelming proportions. I'm not starting from scratch, after all. The time is right. Without hesitation, here's a plan:

1. I will reestablish contact with him. I will find the right words. I will submit to the situation. I will be guided by vision. I will submerge into objectivity for all encounters. I have great faith in myself. I can do it if I want. The effort will be made. There is no way I can fail. The strictly defined results are as follows:

(A) My relationship with Dad will be restored, and

(B) The book will, in turn, be written. I have a theme to my impending spiritual travels. It is my own growth. I will find a way to grow, to learn. I am going on a sort of mission, but a mission to learn, not to teach. I cannot avoid coming back anything less than enriched.

All this is psychological preparation for my confrontation with Dad. I must not try to make him understand me. This is his ship; he's captain. He says "Jump," I'll say "How high?" My strongest weapon will be my unswerving willingness to compromise. We may have radically different perspectives, but I will yield to his reality because the situation is worth the effort. I am not exposing myself to threatening forces. For all his chest-thumping, he has only my best interest at heart. That is no minor point. Out of respect for that it will be no great sacrifice to defer to his wishes. It will be my honor to humble myself to him. He is an intelligent, highly accomplished man who, despite all our differences, loves me very much. The situation demands my respect. In reality, my father *does* deserve it.

Am I being insincere? Is this a facade? Yes and no. No, I am not being insincere; yes, this is a facade. It is the kind of facade that is a very real part of my father's world. It is the pomp-and-circumstance routine that is so integral to my father's perspective. He asks to be respected because he deserves to be respected. He does not ask for a running discourse on his right to ask to be respected. I really do now understand that our conflicts in the past arose from my inability to project myself into his position.

My father is a good man who I simply don't understand. But I don't need to clinically understand him to respect him. As I have so clearly learned, reality is not so much something to be understood as it is something to be adapted to. What if I just accept the reality of my father; what real compromises would he ask of me? None. At this point, writing this book is the only way I know to show my father the respect I know he deserves. And after all he's done for me, what right do I have to deny him what little I have to offer? My respect.

What was at stake was not just a book but a relationship. My decision to recontact my father was my duty. It did not depend upon whether or not this book would have to be abandoned but on whether or not my relationship with my father would have to be scrapped. I knew it was worth the effort. The book would be a record of that effort, but the effort itself was primary. The book represented something. What I was confronting was an empty canvas or blank piece of paper in my life. My inspiration to fill it was coming from what I had thought the most unlikely of sources: from my father.

I knew I had to go back to Rhode Island not just to write but to *live* the book. If things turned out badly and I couldn't grow together with him, then I could always change the title to *I Hate My Fascist Swine Father.* Somehow, I sensed it would not have quite the same appeal. So I set my sights on growing together with him, knowing that the nature of the highly structured and regimented approach to rewriting the reciprocal chapters would set the stage for living the rest of it.

The book would be a sort of gift to my father. The inspiration behind it was really no more complex or profound than the inspiration one might have for sending one's father a greeting card on Father's Day. But it would take a lot of greeting cards to unravel the communicational morass in which we had become trapped. The book would be a simple thanks to him for the gift of life. I wanted to show my father, with the book and with my life, that I appreciated the values he had given me. I felt it was important for him to know this, certainly as important as it had been to let him know I am gay.

It wasn't until I picked up the phone that I had my first doubts. What if he hates me for the way I acted? What if this bridge has been torn down long ago? What if he laughs and then hangs up on me? I slammed the receiver back down. Then, after a brief moment of sheer terror, I picked the phone back up and punched in his Rhode Island phone number, urgently mouthing the words *now or never*. I held my breath as the number rang. I had written down the first words I was going to say to him. I got them from a magazine article on how to get along better with your father. The words became meaningless in the split second when I heard his voice on the other end and I just said a resigned, "Hello, this is your son."

My senses rose, attuned to evaluating the slightest nuances of tone in his immediate reply. He had no way of preparing for the call at this time. Even after close to two years, my voice was not the voice of a stranger, however. It had been ingrained permanently in his consciousness as the voice of his child. He responded by simply stating my name with a lull of instinctive parental reassurance. "Aaron." With that, I knew he had not written me off.

The conversation did not last for more than ten minutes, but with that phone call the courses of our lives crossed paths for the first time in nearly two years. Three weeks later, in October of 1988, our lives would cross paths again in Rhode Island, because in that ten minutes we made plans to meet face-to-face to finish this book.

GROWING TOGETHER

I never thought I would feel the same sense of wonder returning to Rhode Island that I felt when I first arrived in California, but three weeks later I got a chill down my back as I stepped on the plane to Rhode Island. I couldn't help but get the feeling that somewhere in my past I was going to find my future.

It was cold when I arrived, especially in contrast to the warm California climate I had left behind. My dad was going to meet me at the airport, but when he was unexpectedly called off to a ship, he sent a limo to pick me up. During the forty-minute drive from the airport to his house, I caught myself looking out at Rhode Island and feeling condescension toward this silly, barren little place. I stopped myself. I knew I had to respect this place; it was part of me. The architecture and landscape of Rhode Island were not as important a part of me as were the overall ambience and attitude of Rhode

Walter H. Fricke

Island, perhaps best exemplified by Providence's own me-
dieval-style cathedral, which the limo was now zooming past.
I felt as if I was looking through the limo window out onto
the past: my past, and a lot of other people's pasts. Every gay
friend I had known in Rhode Island had left. Even my sister
had left. One of the last human ties I had to this place was
my father. And like my father, Rhode Island would always
be there in the recesses of my consciousness.

My dad already had returned home from his piloting job
by the time I arrived. He walked out to the driveway to greet
me. I extended my arm, grasped his hand firmly, and stepped
forward slightly without losing eye contact with him. He knew
I was stiffly following Jim Barry's rules of handshaking, so
instead of stepping forward slightly, he pulled me in close
and said, "Give your dad a hug."

Aaron W. Fricke

That broke the ice. The rest of the evening was not spent catching up on the events of the past two years, it was spent making plans on how to complete the book in the next three weeks. No clearly defined reason for this reconciliation had been established except the completion of this book. It was its completion that would represent our moving on.

So a work schedule was set up almost immediately. Between twelve-thirty and two-thirty in the afternoon we would sit together and review the already-written material. Then I would spend the rest of the afternoon working independently rewriting and reassembling the reviewed material. After dinner, one more hour would be devoted to discussion, during which I would take notes. I would spend the rest of the evening writing, and finally before bed, I would determine the direction in which the next day's discussions would go.

This was the routine we intended to follow for the next three weeks. It was a rigid approach to a reconciliation, but we intuitively sensed that it was the only way.

The major thought we had in mind was that we would share some of the thoughts and experiences in our own relationship with parents and gay people who might be able to relate to or even benefit from what we had learned. He would speak to the parents; I would speak to the children; and somehow or other, we hoped we would actually be speaking to each other. Here's what we came up with during our first week.

ACCEPTING YOUR GAY CHILDREN

by Walter

When a parent witnesses something threatening happen to his child, the incident will remain indelible in the parent's memory. I have permanent recall of one such threatening incident that happened when my son was four years old.

Aaron had been walking just inches in front of me as we entered the breezeway behind our local pharmacy. He reached for what he thought was the door to the pharmacy and in the blink of an eye was tumbling head over heels down into what was actually a darkened cellar. He fell so suddenly that I did not have a chance to grab hold of him. My brain was working a bit faster than my arms, because as I ran down the stairs, I projected calling an ambulance and perhaps applying splints to him before the ambulance arrived. By the time I reached the bottom of the stairs, however, Aaron was standing firmly upright, unscathed. This was the first time I had encountered the feeling of losing Aaron to a darkened unknown, but certainly not the last.

As a young boy, Aaron was bright and inquisitive and had a talent for attracting people's attention. He was the kind of kid who was known by everyone. When picking him up from school, I could ask any teacher, any kid, and even the school custodian where Aaron could be found; they would all know.

Aaron seemed to have a certain understanding of his uniqueness. This very well could be due to something as simple as the choice of his name, which set him apart from the other kids. There were not three other Aarons as there might have been three other Billys or Jimmys. When anyone addressed Aaron, they were talking to the one and only Aaron. This may be a simplistic explanation, but for whatever reason, Aaron was Aaron . . . and he knew it.

Aaron's awareness of his distinct individuality was hardly a negative characteristic in my eyes. In fact, my parental instincts told me that this acute self-recognition was most likely a productive trait that would reflect positively on Aaron's potential. As a parent, I could ask for little more than a child who had the ability to realize and pursue that potential . . . except, maybe, that Aaron not be gay.

The job of a parent, to a large extent, is to mold a child. When a parent's mold becomes too confining, it can be unhealthy. The absence of any positive parental guidance is just as negative. I had this understanding as I raised Aaron with the idea that life has a lot to offer when one makes sure to look. In molding Aaron, I simply tried to expose him to as much as possible. I often took him to the Boston Museum of Science, intent on showing him there was more to the world than met the eye; more to see than our small Rhode Island hometown could show. Before bedtime, I would read

My father being held by his father (left), and my father holding me (below).

to my son from a topic in the encyclopedia. Homosexuality was never one of those topics.

That Aaron would be heterosexual was simply and indisputably taken for granted. When Aaron was about nine, a scene took place at the same local pharmacy as previously mentioned. He had spotted a cute little girl exiting, so he made his way to the door, held it open, and smiled at the girl as she walked by. Later, when he turned to me confused about why he felt tenderness toward her, I explained that these were the first stirrings of appreciation of the opposite sex. He looked perplexed at this, and I did not expand on it at the time. Still, his actions served as confirmation to me of a budding nine-year-old's impending heterosexuality.

I saw that Aaron was never overly active like many other young boys were. He was always especially timid about engaging in sports. This did not seem to be cause for alarm, considering that as a child I tended toward the cerebral and was not overly active, either. Of course, our father and son relationship was headed for the test bound to occur in all growing parent/child relationships: adolescence.

Adolescence gives rise to a generation gap between parents and their children. Generation gaps do not merely imply a distance in years, however. If that were the case, generation gaps would occur between parents and their two-year-old children. Generation gaps invariably arise during the child's adolescence, that most memorable and classic period of life that so clearly establishes each and every one of us as distinct and separate identities.

Up until adolescence, Aaron never seemed to have any problems expressing his identity. Then, around the time my son was thirteen or fourteen, I noticed him withdrawing. He shut himself up in his room. No friends came to visit. He had no peer group to speak of. It was as if Aaron was ex-pressing his teen rebellion through total apathy.

The last interest he held into adolescence was his *Wacky* magazine (a bimonthly satire he created, which he distributed at school). The articles became increasingly loaded with sex-ual innuendo, and complaints from other parents were reg-istered with the school administration. When he went so far as to depict two "invisible dog" leashes engaged in sexual intercourse, I *had* to exercise some editorial control over the magazine's content. He considered this censorship, and the magazine died, as did something inside of Aaron.

I knew that something was wrong as I watched the identity that had been such an intrinsic part of Aaron's boyhood slip away. I saw him becoming secluded, but I didn't know how to break down the barriers. I searched for a possible expla-nation for what seemed like an out-of-the-ordinary problem, even for an adolescent. In my struggle to understand, I won-dered whether Aaron's indifference might be caused by some form of drug abuse. At one point when I found him alone in his room writing on his bedroom mirror with a Magic Marker, I was sure he was having a bad trip. So he was placed in a juvenile center and given a battery of tests. The tests showed Aaron was not using any drugs. Homosexuality is not detectable through blood tests.

After that, he withdrew even more. He gained weight dras-tically and became hostile to any sort of intervention. I felt helpless as I watched my son balloon to a staggering 217 pounds and stay that way for a couple of years.

Then, around the time Aaron was turning seventeen, he introduced me to his first new friend in years. This friend was so obviously gay that I felt compelled to warn Aaron. He said that he didn't really know the guy that well, so I let the matter rest. It was not so much later that Aaron began dieting to lose weight. Then he started trotting more gay friends into the house, too. When I approached him about these friends, he said he was aware that his friends were gay but that he felt sorry for them when other people picked on them. The mixture of emotions that this caused me should be obvious.

I had fears. I knew the libido of a seventeen-year-old boy is strong and I wondered whether these homosexuals might be availing themselves and taking advantage of the natural curiosity of Aaron's own seventeen-year-old libido. I thought it entirely possible that these boys could be plying my son with some sort of favors. Were they doing his homework for him? I wondered. (Aaron's grades were, after all, improving at this point.) My worst fear was that Aaron might be some kind of sexual puppet to these boys.

Then, just a year and a half after Aaron had introduced me to his first gay friend, he was sitting on the witness stand during his lawsuit to win the legal right to attend the senior prom with that same gay friend. As I sat in the courtroom the day Aaron gave testimony, I experienced a revelation. The identity Aaron seemed to have lost during adolescence came flooding back right before my eyes. He was becoming a man. He was standing up for something he really believed in. As I looked at Aaron from the back of that courtroom, I felt proud. Aaron was nobody's puppet. I could look at my son for the first time since his childhood and proudly say as a father, "That's my son . . . that's *my* son."

I certainly was not *proud* of the fact that Aaron was gay. And it is inconceivable for me to take pride in homosexuality because Aaron is gay. It was his ability to stand up for something he believed in of which I was proud. I have never really been able to look at Aaron from the same perspective I view homosexuality. To expect any parent to look at their child with that kind of objectivity is simply asking too much. In many ways, empathizing with your own gay children is virtually impossible. I have a difficult time integrating Aaron's identity as a homosexual with Aaron's identity overall. I recognize this as a mental block, but one that most people will have when thinking of their own gay child.

I do not have so much difficulty understanding the plight of *other* young gay people. Aaron has given me the chance to peruse the bagfuls of letters he received in response to his talk-show appearances, and perhaps 90 percent of the letters were from young gay people who told their own stories about what it felt like growing up gay. Aaron used many of these letters as reference for *Reflections of a Rock Lobster*, and modeled that book as an extended letter to all of those young gay people who sought help. Other parents might glean some objective insight on growing up gay from Aaron's book. And paradoxically, my best insight comes from the letters of other parents' gay kids. It is on those letters that I base the following comments, knowing only subconsciously that many aspects of those letters are very similar to Aaron's own "growing up gay" story.

The recurrence of major themes in these young people's letters amazed me. There was the specifically expressed thought that they had seen Aaron on television and no longer felt isolated and alone. For many, Aaron was the first openly gay person they ever had encountered. As they watched him telling his story about growing up gay, they felt their own stories had been vicariously validated. There was a remarkable consistency among the stories they related.

Most commonly, the letters detailed accounts of hostility, from locker-room taunts to severe beatings, sometimes from parents. I got the feeling that before Aaron, these kids had *no* one to talk to. It would seem that about the time they reached puberty, they realized they were gay, they felt estranged from society, and they felt helpless. These fundamental struggles may not be so different from our own heterosexual feelings during puberty, except for the one essential difference: These kids were dealing with being gay.

How are parents who are raised in a society that says even "normal" sex is something to be ashamed of supposed to understand what these kids go through? Perhaps the best way to start is by acknowledging that it very well could be that the gender attraction your children feel is as strong as the one you feel. If you take the intimidation and shame you felt about your own sexuality during puberty and then multiply it a thousand fold, you can probably get a clearer picture of how a young homosexual must feel about his or hers.

You must stop there in your clinical analysis of your gay child's sexuality. It may sound awful, but you must sanitize your thoughts of your gay children and separate them from your thoughts about homosexual acts. Up until you found out your child was gay, homosexuality was probably on the periphery of your concerns, and it is perhaps best that it stay there. It's true that being gay is bound to make growing up much harder for your children, but it really is their own personal challenge. Hopefully, they will understand, or come to understand, that as hard as it was for them to look at themselves while growing up gay and say "I am gay," it is a thousand times more difficult for you to look at yourself and say "My child is gay."

That doesn't mean you love them any less. You must love them as the individuals you've always loved, capable of every emotion you are capable of. If loving another person of the same sex is what they lean toward, then the least you can do is be thankful they are capable of love.

ACCEPTING YOUR HETEROSEXUAL PARENTS

by Aaron

My father taught me the intrinsic simplicity of having knowledge and the inevitable complexities of life that arise without it. For example, he removed the inner compartment of an ice tray once and asked me to fill it and place it in the freezer. I filled the tray basin and started to walk across the room. I fumbled to the left and a little water splashed out. Then I tipped to the right and more water was lost. By the third wobble, two-thirds of the water was on the floor. I turned to him, expecting to see an angry expression, but he was already at my feet sponging up the mess. He told me to try it again, this time with the inner compartment. Then I found I was able to walk briskly back and forth to the freezer without spilling a drop. It seemed like magic, but it wasn't. It was my dad's magical way of teaching an eight-year-old the concept of ballasting. He was familiar with that concept, since he had spent years studying to become a ship's pilot. He started at

King's Point Academy and went on to get his master's degree from Georgetown University.

A lot of the things my dad taught me—from how to bowl to how to overcome fear of the unknown—took on a particular relevance in my life. As a matter of fact, before my father could teach me how to bowl, he had to teach me why I was afraid. I had never been bowling when I was nine years old and was a little scared when my dad suggested we go. Sensing my natural timidity, he used these words to encourage me to seek out new experiences: "You'll always be afraid of something the first time you do it. That's only human nature. But the only way to conquer this fear is to do it."

These were pretty adult words to be sharing with a nine-year-old kid, but to this day these are the words that echo through my mind with every challenge I struggle to overcome. Back then, they convinced me I should give bowling a shot.

My dad would watch me intensely each time I threw the bowling ball down the aisle. Then he would offer advice on how to improve my score. He told me not to watch the pins so much as the closer arrow marks on the lane. If it was a strike I wanted, he suggested aiming for the arrow just to the right of the middle one. He taught me the importance of follow-through. On one occasion when my attention drifted and I began throwing one gutter ball after another, my father took me aside and said, "Relax, son . . . don't worry that you can't make a strike every time. Just remember my words each time you get up there, and keep the focus on what you're trying to do. If you do this, you'll be performing to the best of your abilities and that's all that really counts."

I noticed then, and know now, that when I follow this advice, I always get a better score.

I felt as if I had a special friend in my dad. Looking back, I realize that his attentiveness nourished my boyhood psyche.

When my actions warranted disciplinary action, however, I got that, too.

Once, when I was in fifth grade, he found out I had "bunked" (a peculiar Rhode Island expression for skipping school). He approached me that evening. Rather than letting on immediately, he decided to take advantage of this excellent opportunity to teach me a valuable lesson. Feigning both ignorance and nonchalance, he asked me whether I had had a good day at school. I was well rehearsed for this question.

"Yeah, I had a good day at school."

He was armed with a follow-up, though.

"Oh, really. How did you do on your English test?"

I was not so well rehearsed for this one.

"English test? Oh, yeah, English test. Um, I aced it."

I tried to turn to walk away.

"Uh-huh. And did you see Jeffrey at school?"

I sensed I was tensing up but knew I had to stay cool or I would arouse my dad's suspicion.

"Jeffrey? Oh yeah, I saw him. We played 'Planet of the Apes' during recess."

"How very interesting. When Jeffrey called before you came home, he said he hadn't seen you all day."

I switched to automatic pilot.

"He did? Oh, well. You know Jeffrey. Ever since he swallowed that pool water last summer, his short-term memory's been shot."

"Now, Aaron, I know you didn't see Jeffrey today, because you didn't go to school."

Dead silence.

"You're grounded for two weeks for skipping school."

Feeling totally humiliated, I turned to walk into my room.

"Now wait just one minute, young man, I'm not through with you yet. It's bad enough that you skipped school, but it's even worse that you lied to me. For that, you get an extra two weeks. That's one month with no phone calls, no movies. You are to come directly home from school, and it's lights out at eight o'clock for the next thirty days. And during that time, I want you to think of the very important thing I am about to say to you. . . . Every lie will lead to another, even bigger lie. Now go to your room."

As much as I tried not to during the long month that followed, I repeatedly thought of my father's words. I'll never forget those words. There is only one thing that my father ever said that I could not figure out. It was "Life is a paradox." I could not assign any relevance to this vague phrase, not in my childhood.

When I was twelve and my father took me aside to explain the facts of life, I reacted with hysterical laughter. It wasn't the mechanics of heterosexual sex that I was laughing at, but more the expression on my father's face as he explained it. He believed that a boy of twelve would naturally have serious questions about this matter. I had few questions. The entire scenario he described was just an abstraction to me because, even at twelve, I was already aware of what gave me sexual pleasure, and what my father described was definitely not it.

I soon learned that there was nothing abstract about these facts of life. They were something a lot of people in the world take seriously every day of their lives. I wondered whether I would someday grow to feel the same way as other people felt about them, but I never did.

Parents with the purest intentions can still be ignorant to the special needs of a gay youth. Oftentimes, parents show distaste toward the subject of homosexuality, or avoid any acknowledgement that homosexuals even exist. These attitudes are pretty commonplace in society. If you were heterosexual, you would probably pick these attitudes up from your parents, just as they probably did from theirs.

Many of their images of gay people come from mass-media portraits of what homosexuals are supposed to be like. They read about one mass-murdering, child-molesting homosexual and they associate this image with all gay people. Such an image is an abstraction to them. Children represent the greatest source of pride in the parental experience. Even though the concept of children being responsible for the future of this earth may seem clichéd to some by now, it has profound meaning to parents. Given this, and all the negative information parents believe about homosexuality, it should not be so hard to understand why your parents are so protective.

They are attempting to shield their family from the threat of homosexuality. The family is shelter. It is the parents' responsibility to protect it. Family unity is considered by many to be the closest type of human bond. What parents sometimes fail to take into account is that no matter how strong the family unit is, there lies a magnificent potential for individual variation within that unit. Diversity is one of the facts of life.

The irony is that the family unit, which ideally would reinforce the individuality of its members, can assume such a fragile identity of its own that individual variation within the group becomes a threat to the group itself. The predicament facing gay youth is that their identity is threatening to the very fabric of the group into which they are born. That is, homosexuality is taboo.

Sometimes parents propagate misconceptions about homosexuality. They may hope that they will sway their children from "becoming" gay. They have a wide variety of these misconceptions to choose from, such as homosexuality is a disease that you can catch if touched by a homosexual; homosexuals travel in wolf packs prowling for young children; homosexuals are unhappy; and so on. All these unfounded beliefs are inappropriate for any child to hear, but they are especially detrimental to the homosexual child.

It cannot be stressed enough times that sexuality is innate and few people choose their sexual preference. Parents may think they have good intentions in trying to direct their children's sexuality with negative images, but this action does not produce the intended results. In their heterosexual children, parents are instilling an unnecessary fear or hatred of gay people. On the other hand, for the homosexual youth who is becoming aware of his or her sexuality, the damage is much worse, because their parents are unwittingly rejecting them.

Although my dad never really demonstrated any blatant homophobia to me, he was not able to recognize the source of my emotional turmoil during adolescence. Around the time I was fourteen and I came to understand that a very real part of myself, my homosexuality, was considered by many to be a personal anomaly, some serious distance occurred between my father and me.

I had learned from my father how to appreciate my unique personal qualities, but stifling them was something altogether new for me. This was something I had to learn on my own and I was scared. I began to feel that I had a big secret to keep from my dad.

By inserting homosexual references into my *Wacky* cartoons, I was subconsciously crying out for some sign of recognition and acceptance. There was no sign. When seventh-grade parents' visitation day arrived, I looked for this sign in his observation of a certain teacher whom all the kids assumed to be gay.

"So-o-o, what did you think of Mr. Black, Dad?" I blurted out with forced nonchalance.

"Well, Mr. Black said you are a good student but that you're not working up to your capabilities."

"Oh . . . but what did you think about *him*, Dad?" I pushed.

My father paused, a bit confused about what I was getting at.

"Well, to tell you the truth, son, he did seem a little on the weird side. Do you think you might do better with a different teacher?"

"No!" I shot back overzealously.

I probed no further. Several other students transferred out of the class during the next week and I knew the reason why.

Soon afterward, I slipped into a kind of communicational coma. I just could not bring myself to share the root of my problems with my father. I was well aware that both my parents thought I was on drugs, but somehow letting them think this was easier than telling them the truth. I was afraid they wouldn't understand. I wasn't even sure if I *wanted* them to understand. Consequently, I decided they never could understand me and I never could understand them. That was a long time ago, however. Since then, I have learned that homosexuality is not a psychological aberration. I have also come to accept that as something my father could never have taught me.

Not understanding your parents is pretty common at one point or another to everyone's experiences growing up. Respect forbids any in-depth critique of the methods my father chose to raise me, so all of this is meant to delineate objectively some of the common denominators that influence all parents. It is not meant to dissect all the things my father did wrong in raising me, but to respectfully recognize that concerning homosexuality all parents have a lot to learn.

The problem is that parents conjure up shame when they think of homosexuality. They have an extremely tough time comprehending gay pride. To your parents, gay pride may seem to be a pride in alien sexual activities. It may be unthinkable for them to respect that.

What parents do not usually understand is that gay pride has nothing to do with a sexual act. Gay pride is really a triumph over years of struggle with prejudice. Gay people are proud of the character it takes to *be* proud to be gay. All this is difficult for parents to sort out.

So give your parents the benefit of the doubt. Don't judge them by what you wish they could or would be like. It's true, there is no law that says you have to be close to your parents just because they're your parents, but don't create extra distance only because they're your parents, either. Don't allow yourself to feel personally hurt by their ignorance, just as you shouldn't feel personally hurt by anyone's ignorance.

You may actually come to like your parents' good points and bad, their insight and their ignorance, their strengths and their weaknesses. These contrasts surely reside within every human being, including yourself. Understanding your heterosexual parents takes a lot of straightforward understanding of yourself.

*   *   *

Things went really smoothly between us that first week. Our writing was progressing steadily and we had relaxed into our work schedule, which would commence every day at 12:30 P.M. At the beginning of the second week, however, I must have become a little too relaxed, because after waking up at 10:00 A.M., exercising, and then showering, I didn't show up at our worktable until 12:44 P.M. My dad was already sitting there, and he quietly watched me shuffling and arranging the work before finally sitting down at 12:48 P.M. At that point, he calmly informed me that the day's work had been canceled due to my tardiness. I was stunned and felt a gripping sense of doom come over the project. I sat there staring at him. He interrupted the silence.

"I want you to understand, son, that I'm doing this to help you."

In my anger of the moment, I really didn't understand. I could, however, see that a lot of what happened in the future would depend on my reaction at that moment. So I squelched my urge to turn the situation into an ordeal by acting like a brat and just said, "Okay, Dad, I trust you because I've met enough people in my life to know the difference between who's out to help me and who's not."

Whatever ground that needed to be declared had been declared. And in its way, not working on the book turned out to, in fact, be work on the book. I experienced in practice the mental attitude that came from yielding to my father. And by so doing, the book work would benefit because I quite literally had to adhere to the established time schedule. I showed up the next day, and all of the proceeding days, promptly at 12:30 P.M. Our work continued.

TELLING YOUR PARENTS YOU'RE GAY

by Aaron

Telling your parents that you are gay, or "coming out" to them, is a brave act that must be prepared for with a lot of prior soul-searching. Sometimes this soul-searching reveals that the wisest thing is to say nothing to your parents. When common sense tells you that you stand to lose more than to gain, this is a perfectly legitimate reason not to tell them.

A strong argument can be made for not coming out to your parents. Many gay people make the conscious choice never to tell their parents, and all that may be missing from their lives is a lot of hardship that might have been caused by coming out. If you have given careful and intelligent thought to the matter and come to the conclusion that coming out to your parents would be a mistake, then you know what is best for you and no one is in a position to tell you that you're wrong.

If, however, you are not so resolute and question whether

My dad took this picture of me (at age six) doing my best to show him I'd learned what he taught me about kicking a football.

or not honesty is, in fact, the best policy, there are many variables you must take into consideration. Are *you* ready? Are *they* ready? Why do you want to tell them? Given their ethnic/religious heritage, how will they be able to assimilate this knowledge into their lives? What do you stand to gain in telling them, or lose by not telling them? Or vice versa, for that matter. For those of you who think you want to tell your parents but are not quite sure, these broad points of self-evaluation may be useful, although not necessarily comprehensive, guidelines.

Discerning whether or not you are ready is a very personal dilemma. There is no universal scale of maturity by which you can gauge yourself. The broadest personal examination of your readiness must start with your personal understanding of what you hope to accomplish. Your own private expectations for growth must take precedence over predictions of your parents' reactions.

Granted, the open line of communication should benefit all parties involved, but in all probability your parents will not see your honesty as greatly commendable right away. Do not justify coming out by imagining that you are doing your parents a great favor by opening up to them. You will be setting yourself up for resentment toward them when they don't respond with sheer gratitude.

It is not a good idea to center your motivation for coming out to your parents on anticipations of their reaction, but it might be best to peripherally prepare for the possibility of some hostility from them once they know. A word of caution: Try at all costs to make sure that hostility does not play a role in your motivation for telling them. In a moment of rage, your homosexuality may seem like the ultimate weapon against your parents. Just remember, that weapon may turn out to be a boomerang that you'll be running from the rest of your life. If you have even a twinge of animosity or resentment when considering whether or not you will tell your parents, do *not* tell them; you are not ready.

You may question whether or not your parents are ready. Have you ever heard your father say something like, "If any of my kids were a deviate, I'd take a submachine gun and kill some innocent people in a shopping mall"? This would be a good clue that he's not ready. Or if your mother has ever referred to homosexuals as "Satan beasts who should be castrated," then she's probably not ready either.

No matter how tame or extreme your parents views of homosexuality may be, you will never be able to predict their views of *you* as a homosexual. A parent with vicious opinions of gay people might turn around and surprise you with unconditional love. The parents who have gay friends and are seemingly open-minded might take you for a turn by wanting to commit suicide when you tell them. Parents are a strange breed, impossible to second-guess. It is not advisable to over-emphasize *their* readiness. Instead, look inward and clearly define your own motivation for telling them. If the time comes and you do decide to tell them, expect the unexpected.

Speaking of the unexpected—there have been many times when people do not have much time to prepare for dealing with their parents. They do not *tell* their parents at all; but, instead, their parents find out. It could happen that you will confide in a brother or sister who, in turn, tells your parents. Or maybe you might get caught having sex, or your parents read a personal letter you've written to a lover. Any one of these situations is going to make dealing with your parents a much more spontaneous kind of interaction. Be careful.

In this type of situation, your parents' panic may fill you with the same feeling of dread they are experiencing. You would probably not be in a position to counter it with level-headedness. They may unconsciously take advantage of your vulnerability. In an effort to get you to "turn straight," they may use scare tactics, such as telling you they would rather be dead than live with your disgrace. Do *not* let this attitude rub off on you. Because even though you can thank your parents for your biological creation, it is now your duty to sustain that entity. And it is of utmost importance that you privately and persistently insist on pride in yourself, in your identity, as a permanent fixture of that sustenance. Try not to confuse their fear of homosexuality with a fear of you, and don't ever let anyone make you feel so ashamed or guilty of your identity that you should want to terminate it.

The most important element of why you should want to tell your parents that you are gay is intangible. It is something that must emanate from within yourself and give you the will and the courage to be straightforward about your homosexuality. You must unravel and conquer all that you have been taught to fear and hate about homosexuality and, consequently, yourself. The most important reason to want to come out to your parents is as simple as human respect. Self-respect is, in fact, the most important reason that you should want to tell them.

I was scared before I confronted my dad. I confronted him one-on-one in a room with soft cushiony chairs that he could sit on (or break his fall with). The one overwhelming feeling I had was a complete confidence that no matter what the outcome, it would be for the best. I was not merely seeking acceptance; I was acting on a need to communicate with him. It was right for me not simply because of honesty for honesty's sake but because it represented the chance, the one revitalizing opportunity for growth. The words came out—"Dad, I'm gay"—and that was it. The occasion did not turn into an ugly moment but, rather, one that he and I both look back upon as a turning point in our relationship, as gut-wrenching as it seemed at the time.

Do not tell your parents you are gay just to be like us, though. You must find your own motivations and your own goals. Trying to pattern yourself exactly after the Aaron and Walter you read about in this book is not a good idea. Coming out to your parents can be an exhausting experience, an experience that anyone who has gone through could write a book about.

SUGGESTIONS ON HOW TO RESPOND

by Walter

Nothing can prepare you for the day when your child comes to you and says "I'm gay." Nothing in your consciousness will allow you to accept that your child could be that way and no words of advice can really cushion the aftereffects once you are told. Perhaps you will have a heterosexual child and be spared from ever hearing those words. Remember, it is also possible to have a gay child and never hear those words. One thing is certain, if your child *is* heterosexual, that child will never come to you and say "I'm straight."

Even if you have suspicions that your child is gay, it will be difficult to work up enough courage to ask "Are you gay?" It may seem easier to ask "You are heterosexual, right?" but fear of a negative response will usually prevent you from inquiring. You may tell yourself that you don't want to know, that it is not important. Yet if it is not important, why does it feel as if you're going to have a stroke when the time comes and those two words "I'm gay" come out of your child's mouth?

You may go through a denial stage first, telling yourself that it isn't true, that it couldn't possibly be true. You may rush to your nearest calendar in hopes of discovering that it is April Fool's Day and this is just your heterosexual child's idea of a cruel joke. What will seem most cruel is if it is not a joke. Deluding yourself isn't going to change the situation. This is one you have to face head-on.

Keep in mind that your child would be gay whether or not you were told. And when you are told, it is with good intentions and innocence. To you, it may seem like a catastrophe, but to your child it is a metamorphosis. You can't be expected to understand that concept right away but you can make a start by accepting that your child has come to terms with a vital aspect of him/herself and *has* to share it with you. It would be unreasonable to expect you to share the enthusiasm, but it is not unreasonable to expect levelheadedness on your part.

When your child reveals his or her homosexuality, you and your child are facing a gigantic moment of truth. Your actions at this moment are bound to be unpredictable. The tragedy is when parents reject or disown their gay child for coming out to them. That act shows a lack of concern for the future. The enormous confusion you feel at the moment you are told is only normal, but there are two basic choices to fall back on in responding to this information: You can either react as you would to a homosexual stranger or you can react as you would to the child you have always loved and cared for. Granted, at the moment you are told, there will be a tendency to feel as though you don't know your child at all. The single most important thought to keep in mind at that moment is that this person is the same one you have always loved and nurtured. Your child will be looking for affirmation of that fact. A negative or violent reaction won't help.

Your parental instincts tell you to punish your children when they do something wrong and to reward them when they do something acceptable. That doesn't work in this case. Though you may have come to believe that homosexuality is not acceptable, your child has done nothing wrong in coming out to you. Punishing your child for this honesty will not change your child's sexual orientation. Just try to acknowledge that it is not realistic to reward the honesty and not sensible to punish it.

In coming out to you, your children have enough confidence in themselves and in you to reveal their homosexuality. It is a major gamble for them because your response is unpredictable. Yet still they feel the need to share this with you. You may not really want them to share it, and may even believe they have done something to deliberately hurt you, but the unavoidable truth is that your children are simply expressing honesty with you. And they are taking risks in doing so.

Serious complications arise when a different scenario occurs. Some children take a malicious tack when coming out to their parents. Perhaps it will happen during an argument. Being informed of your child's homosexuality is never easy, but coming to this realization during an argument is infinitely more difficult. You'll feel struck down even if your child comes out to you in a civil manner, but under hostile circumstances the emotions are compounded. Yes, it is unfair for your child to make this disclosure with hostility. Yes, your child is playing a game with you and has just pulled the trump card. No, you never wanted to play this game, but you have been swept up in it and are now in trouble.

You must not play this game; you cannot win. Do not even

attempt to continue the conversation, because your interactions will inevitably lead back toward antagonism. At this point you feel backed into a corner and ferocious. Your only defense, however, is to say nothing. Accept the situation and walk away. (Then you can look up the closest chapter of Parents and Friends of Lesbians and Gays for someone to talk to*.)

On the other hand, when you are confronted in a civil manner, your child is in many ways displaying respect for you. He or she is being honest, and honesty is, after all, something you have probably always strived to instill in your child. He or she is hoping that you can cope with this truth. In effect, your child is trusting you with a great secret. It's only fair that you respect that trust.

Responding to your gay child is not an exact science. Even if it were, it is unlikely that many parents would care to study it. It is impossible to cover all bases in one chapter and describe the "right" way to respond to your child. The only responsible solution is to listen without rancor. Most of responding to your child's homosexuality relies upon love and intuition.

At age eighteen, Aaron took me aside and with a serious vocal intonation tried to set the stage for what he was about to say. I suspected it was something momentous, but I didn't expect to hear those words. I have always dealt with problems through my own rationality or turned to God for guidance. My reaction when Aaron told me he was gay was probably a combination of both influences. I cried. It was a spontaneously honest reaction, reminiscent of the same honesty with which Aaron had confronted me.

---

*For information, write to P-Flag at 1012 14th St. NW, Washington, D.C. 20038, or call them at (202) 638-4200.

Days afterward, I overcame the initial shock and realized my son was the same son I always had loved. Because of this, I was able to take Aaron out to a restaurant and respond to his homosexuality by saying, "I never thought I'd be sitting in a restaurant with a homosexual telling him I love him." Try it on your kid!

* * *

Midway into the second week, we were sifting through some of the garbage I had previously written in an attempt to create a picture-perfect heterosexual parent/gay child relationship when we ran across this:

> The metaphor for Aaron and Walter's relationship is that of a sunflower thriving in the light of truth. But it should be remembered that different plants thrive best under different lights. A fern, for example, will thrive best with some cloaking from direct light. You might be wise to first figure out if your relationship with your parents is a sunflower or a fern, or the whole thing could mushroom out of proportion.

We were in hysterics. It was the first good laugh we had shared in many years. He kept playfully teasing me by asking whether this was going to be a scientific treatise correlating various flora and fauna to us. (And which one was homosexual, the sunflower or the fern?) He parodied the title of my first book, saying this one could be called *Plantations of a Fernius Maximus*. We laughed until tears streaked our faces. It turned out to be the first good cry we shared in years, too.

This episode served to release a lot of unspoken tensions between us. My written words represented just how much faith I had lost in our real father/son relationship. Now by laughing at it and writing "Yikes!" over the text of that paragraph, I realized we had already come a long way.

PRAYING FOR CHANGE

by Aaron

I believe in God. For those who do not know, being a homosexual and believing in God are not mutually exclusive. For those who do know, please excuse this triteness.

I know very clearly what God means to me. To describe this personal understanding might be a bit too prophetic for this book, however. The usual platitudes "God is good" and "God is love" will suffice, but they do not encompass the profound thoughts I have toward my concept of God. My understanding of God emanates from my intrinsic beliefs in everything. The existence of God is not something I feel comfortable debating, as if the subject in question was the Abominable Snowman. To me, clinically analyzing the presence of God is like trying to prove the existence of love scientifically. Using facts and data to prove that love exists could only dilute its true essence rather than materialize it. In my opinion, the same holds true for God.

Here I am at age seven, looking a bit skeptical about the Easter bunny.

I am not so reserved about my opinions of institutionalized religion. My thoughts are based on my informal familiarity with the Judeo-Christian society in which I was raised. I do not devote myself to any of the various denominations of Judaism or Christianity, however, because I have seen religious people's beliefs become so closely associated with these groups that the groups themselves become a vital link to people's perception of God. This aspect of religious institutions scares me.

I sense a double standard at the heart of the Judeo-Christian tradition. In these groups, there are commandments of right and wrong that pertain to the individual, while the actions of the group as a whole are not judged by the same articulately stated standards (i.e., "Thou shalt not kill," while capital punishment gains popularity). In fact, I believe that while the animal instinct of individual members needs to be squelched in order for the group to survive, a collective venting of animal instinct also seems to be crucial to group survival. There seems to be a specific need to abandon collective conscience.

The whole idea is perhaps better left for exploration in a college term paper, but it is presented here to explain my personal apprehensions about religious institutions. It is my experience that the groups I have encountered—from Cub Scouts to gay rap groups—always have had an uncanny talent for rationalizing some actions that my private conscience cannot. When actions are justified by invoking the approval of God, however, I am sickened. Thus, prayer and God are steadfastly solitary experiences for me.

Yet I find comfort in the concept of a group. It's the group psychology that I sometimes find disagreeable. For instance, I thank God for the chance to have come to understand that I am not alone in the world as a homosexual. Then there are those occasions when I have encountered other gay people who expect me to share their racism simply because I'm white, and I cannot help but wonder if I am, in some ways, still alone.

My philosophical outlook is undeniably influenced by the teachings of Christianity. Christianity glorifies the life of a man who was crucified, the popular form of capital punishment in His time. His story is that of an innocent man killed in the name of that which was thought to be good for His society. In my opinion, the image of this man dying on the cross is supposed to illustrate the hideous crime that His society committed by murdering him in His innocence. I interpret an unequivocal message in the story. The profound lesson I have learned from Christianity is that a society, although giving every appearance of good intention, can actually be undermining everything God stands for.

I sincerely believe that the image of Jesus Christ has become a paradox, used by some men to force submission to *their* ideals, not God's. I believe Jesus Christ spoke the word of God and was killed for it. I am afraid, however, that too many people take this message at face value and simply do not speak the words of God out of a fear of getting nailed for it as Jesus was. To me, the example Jesus set was in His *life* not His death. I have often wondered whether we are divided into two groups of people: those who glorify the brutally graphic image of a dying Jesus as a way of holding authority over others, and those who obey this authority from the fear of being treated as Jesus was.

I am not smug about this. I pray to God that there is not even a shred of truth to it. For I know that if there are those who look at the crucified body of Jesus and interpret it as the price one pays for not conforming, then if we all look very closely at that cross we will see ourselves.

It is because of my experience with God's will that I have come to these dramatic conclusions. When I was in my teens and thought of my homosexuality as a dirty little secret that I shared only with God, I prayed for change. I prayed that God would make me heterosexual. God answered my prayers in a more profound way than by making me heterosexual, however. I stayed true to my identity and God showed me a new understanding of the world in which that identity was grounded. And at those times when I feel that world leaves something to be desired, I do not pray for sweeping social reforms, because I believe there are some things one must pray to God for and other things that require a little personal sweat. In my opinion, sweeping social reform belongs to the latter category.

So before I ever pray to be heterosexual in order to be accepted, I remember that God accepts only those who are true to themselves. Before I ever equate heterosexuality with happiness, I remind myself that there are a lot of unhappy heterosexuals in the world. If my homosexuality is something that makes my father one of those unhappy heterosexuals, I do not pray to be heterosexual. Because I know that if I can show myself as the decent, hardworking person my father raised me to be, then his happiness is not something for which I will have to pray.

PRAYING FOR CHANGE

by Walter

There are two sides of me and both of them hope that deep within Aaron there is a latent heterosexual screaming to be free. There is my practical-minded side, which offers one solution to liberate Aaron's alter-ego. My son, however, disregards, as a waste of his time and my money, my standing offer to hire a female prostitute for him. My other side is the God-fearing side, which believes that when all else fails, try the strength of prayer. This is the side that goes to bed at night praying that Aaron will not be gay the next morning. Perhaps it is best at this point to address what prayer and God mean to me.

My concept of God is that of a controlling consistency at the center of a totally complex and bewildering universe. I frequently turn to God with thanks for the good things provided me, such as my health. Although I have never turned to God with thanks for my heterosexuality, I *do* turn to God in concern about Aaron's homosexuality.

For me, the line that distinguishes heterosexuality from homosexuality does not divide good from bad. Moreover, my fear is that the division between heterosexuality and homosexuality separates happiness from unhappiness. It is as instinctive for me to need to pray for Aaron to change as it is for Aaron to need to take pride in himself. I see the hatred toward homosexuals, and naturally I wish my son was not a part of that targeted group.

Perhaps there are gay people who may resent me for not carrying banners on a crusade for acceptance of homosexuality, but I must tell the truth as I feel it. Most parents will never be able to stop praying for their gay child's sexuality to change. Praying for change is, after all, a perfectly innocuous act. If my attitude toward Aaron's homosexuality seems harsh and nonaccepting, consider that there are parents who, in their desire to change their gay children, do not stop at prayer.

There are psychologists and religious organizations that prey on the vulnerability of parents and offer a step-by-step treatment for the eradication of a child's homosexuality. Such treatments have been known to go so far as to include aversion shock therapy. Tampering with a mind this way is unproven territory and to do so against someone's will borders on the brink of cruelty. Besides, results from such experimentation are bound to be saturated with slanted interpretations. When it comes to changing the sexuality of your gay children, the only humane recourse appears to be prayer.

Whether a child is heterosexual or homosexual, there are certain universal prayers that a parent will have. There is probably not one of you who does not pray for your child's health. And now, with the current specter of sexually transmitted diseases, it would seem that you have a few extra prayers to say for your gay children. A healthy general prayer that all parents can have for their children's activities regarding everything from engaging in sex to crossing the street is that their children exercise a little common sense.

When dealing with your child's homosexuality, it is difficult to avoid turning to God and asking whether this is the result of parental mistakes you made while raising your child. This is the heaviest burden that all parents of gay people have to carry at one point or another. When you consider this question, you have the opportunity to seize as much objectivity as is parentally possible. You can start by asking yourself *why* you wonder whether it is your fault that your child is gay. You think it is your fault because that is what you have been taught to think. It is a widely believed theory that a child's homosexuality is the parents' fault. People often say that homosexuality is the result of a domineering mother and a weak and unassertive father. Are you to accept this as gospel truth even when it is not at all true? Of course not. You must try to understand that, just like your children, you have been pegged into a socially predetermined slot. Like your children, you must also struggle with shame. The difference is that you don't have to deal with actually being a homosexual, too. Because this is not a minor difference, it prevents your thoughts from ever becoming perfectly aligned with your children's struggle.

There is, however, something you can take into account when you think in terms of sheer numbers. For every homosexual in the world, there are two parents. So that makes an awful lot of people struggling to overcome the "shame of homosexuality." If each and every parent can overcome this shame enough to love their children as God surely wants them to, would there really be such a large majority of people who hate homosexuals?

This is just something to mull over. It won't provide answers to all your questions. Only God can really help you with that. One serious question you are likely to ask is this: Does God love my child any less because my child is gay? I asked this question immediately and received an answer almost as soon: God does not love in measures.

God is protective. God loves. God protects the family. Because I believe all this, I have to ask why God allowed Aaron to be gay. I have to ask why God allowed the very last member of the Fricke family to be a homosexual. Sometimes praying to God leaves more questions than it provides answers. Perhaps the old adage "God works in strange and mysterious ways" applies best here.

I don't pray only for changes in Aaron; I pray for some changes in myself, too. I ask God to help me be more accepting and less caring of whether or not Aaron is gay. God has answered my prayers to an extent. Instead of going to bed *every* night praying for Aaron to change as in the past, now it is more like every other night, sometimes every third night; sometimes even weeks at a time go by. At this point, if Aaron became heterosexual overnight, I would seriously consider entering the priesthood. That Aaron has found the strength within himself to overcome the negative attitudes he has encountered shows me that God is answering some of my prayers.

Although collaborating on this book is not exactly a calling for me, I do feel it is a way of extending myself to other parents rather than leaving them alone to their prayers. Reaching out to other people and sharing constructive ideas is an application of the love God represents to me.

I just remember that God has an infinite wisdom of all things that happen, and I accept. Even before I knew Aaron was gay, I prayed that he could simply retain the integrity with which I tried to raise him. When I found out about

Aaron's homosexuality, I just prayed that God would show me a sign that he was one of the homosexuals in this world who have the qualities of sincerity, honesty, reliability, intelligence, resourcefulness, and common sense from which integrity arises. In really important matters, God has yet to let me down.

* * *

By sticking to our routine, we were getting quite a bit written. The only change in the routine was that the nightly discussion during which I took notes evolved into a nightly walk during which we talked but I took no notes. We grew comfortable enough just to spend this free time together. We were developing a new kind of bond on these walks. We would have conversations, but hardly soul-searching or profound ones. Sometimes we would talk about the weather. It occurred to me that even this simplest form of interaction was of great substance. That is, I began to think that any form of communication, even nonverbal, might actually be the highest form as long as it fostered growth. So I treated these walks with my father, even the ones when I felt he was speaking another language, with the utmost reverence. We were growing further apart, yet closer.

In the middle of the third week, we were on our nightly walk when he noticed I seemed somewhat frazzled.

"What is it, son, is something wrong?"

"Yeah, kind of. The day before I left California, I towed my dead car down to the junkyard. The place was already closed, so I left the pink slip with my friend Doug. He promised me he'd take care of selling it to them the next day and then send me the money. I called him a week ago and he said he sent it, but it's not here yet."

"Oh, Aaron . . . you should know better than to trust these gay people."

He said this with a conciliatory tone, but the words hit me like a clenched fist. As much as I would not deny that my father had a place in my life, I could likewise not deny that it was my own life to live. I needed to say a few words for my own personal comfort.

"Dad, I don't need you to acknowledge this, but please try in your heart to understand that I am capable of making my own decisions. If I was wrong in trusting Doug, please grant me the privilege of finding it out for myself."

"Okay, Aaron, you have the right to make your own decision. But when all is said and done, don't say I didn't tell you so."

In the past, this situation would have deteriorated into an argument that bounced from one heated debate to another as we tried to prove our own perspectives to be right. Now we were satisfied with just stating our own perspectives without feeling they had to be proved. Even so, I dreaded the possibility that he could be right about trusting Doug. I was wondering whether I had been betrayed by my friend, and my dad only made the situation harder by implying that I was gullible about the real ways of the world. I found myself in a struggle to retain my renewed confidence.

The events of the next day made me feel even worse. First, the check from Doug did not arrive. Then, as I was brushing my teeth, my false tooth somehow got accidentally knocked off the edge of the sink into the basin. For some reason, the sink stop had been removed and before I had a chance to grab the tooth, it was swept down with the running water. I would have to go without the tooth until a plumber could get out to the house.

I worked on the book the rest of the day, but the absence of my tooth proved to be a strain. It wasn't merely my vanity that had been threatened; it was as if a part of me had been grabbed and dragged into the Rhode Island sewage system. I thought that Rhode Island was, in spirit, relentless in its effort to have a part of me for itself. To my dad, the situation simply reminded him that this was the same flip tooth inside the same person it had been placed in years ago. The next morning when the tooth was returned, I felt a great sense of relief; and as I calmed down, I realized I had, as usual, melodramatized a bit, especially considering that when this had happened to me once in California, I had some equally absurd analogy for it then, too.

I got another nice surprise that morning. The letter from Doug arrived with the money for the junked car. I went over to my dad and just held the check up for him to look at. I couldn't help but feel a bit self-satisfied as he stood there red-faced looking at the check. Nothing was said about the incident while we worked on the book the rest of the day. But later, on our walk that night, I decided to confront the subject lightly.

"Do you still think all gay people are irresponsible liars, Dad?"

"*Most*, Aaron, I said most gay people are liars, not all."

"Dad, can you just tell me why it was so easy to condemn *most* gay people on no evidence, and not so easy to have praise for one even when the evidence is right in front of you?"

"Okay, okay, Aaron. You were right; I was wrong. You have every right to say 'I told you so.' "

"No, that's okay, Dad. You're only human. You're entitled to make a mistake every once in a great while."

Perhaps he had underestimated the gravity his words

had—or perhaps not. Because in a roundabout way, his challenging of my faith actually strengthened it. He had reinforced my spirit the way a father might bolster his son's physical stamina with a challenge to a game of one-on-one basketball. We were, indeed, growing together. And we had grown together in more than one way. We had both grown as individual human beings while apart, but the more we grew as individuals, the closer we had grown together. As much as I hesitate to resort to botanical analogies at this point, we were, in fact, like two trees that grow together simultaneously yet independent of each other—upward, while their roots grow physically closer together—intertwining. We had grown because he had learned to see the adult as well as the child in me; and I had learned to see the child as well as the adult in him.

By this point, it was well into the third week and we were just days away from the deadline. I was rushing to finish as much writing as possible. As my father stepped to the side and watched me go full-tilt-boogie typing at the computer, he could hardly believe that he was watching the same kid who rarely said a word until the age of three. He was aware that I was writing this book in part to show him respect, but through all the hard work I was putting into this book, he felt I was gaining something much more important, *self*-respect. That was all he really cared about. He continued watching me at the keyboard and didn't even realize I was aware of his presence until I suddenly turned away from our work and said, "Dad, do you think this book could be our baby . . . our child?"

"I don't know, Aaron. That sounds a little perverse to write into this kind of book."

"Maybe you're right. But then again, maybe it's a birth from our spirit . . . from our souls."

I turned right back to the work as if it had never been interrupted. He was no longer afraid for my future as he had been in the past. Watching me hard at work on a second book made him feel as though God was answering his prayers right before his eyes. I was no longer oblivious to the fact that I was going to have to put forth real energy and use my talents to get by in the world. He finally felt as if he had gotten to know me—not all my homosexual friends or my sexual details, but just me. Every parent wants to get to know their child, but when homosexuality is an obstacle to that, it is so painful to get around. He thought to himself that it might be nice if I was heterosexual, but he knew that just because I wasn't, he had not lost me. Because after all the tumultuous emotions had come to rest, he genuinely believed that I had become a respectable human being who had not tumbled into a darkened unknown. Regardless of my sexual orientation, I was standing spiritually upright, unscathed.

For all the frenzied work we were doing, it had taken the entire three weeks just to get the reciprocal sections rewritten and reassembled. By the time the last day of the three weeks had arrived, it was clear that I was going to have to finish the rest of it in California. As we set out on our walk that night, we realized it was the last walk we would take while in the process of writing this book. I finally had the courage to confront a few of the things I knew deserved attention.

"Dad, have you ever hated me, I mean, just hated me?"

"No, Aaron. I have never hated you. You're my son; I could never hate you. Why are you asking me this? Have you ever hated me?"

I hesitated.

"Um, well . . . there was a time when I thought I did."

"It's okay, son. You don't have to tell me about it. If I had

had a father myself, maybe I would have recognized that there comes a time when a kid has to rebel against his father. You see, I never had a father to love *or* to hate. I guess wanting to have a father has been the one romantic notion I've entertained all my life."

"I want to ask you something point-blank, Dad. What went through your mind when you went to jail instead of letting go of your money?"

"Oh, now I see. You hated me for *that*, didn't you?"

"I don't know. I know how I looked at it then and I know how I've come to look at it now. I'm sorry, I shouldn't have brought it up."

"No, Aaron. I'm glad you did. I would like to answer. But let me ask you a question before I do. Do you think that if I was a billionaire I would have just conceded and handed over one hundred thousand dollars?"

"Huh?" I wasn't sure what he was getting at.

"I bet you think that one hundred thousand dollars would mean a lot less to me if I was a billionaire. But let me tell you that if I *was* a billionaire, and your mother and her lawyers were asking for only *one* dollar, I still wouldn't have given it to them. The whole point, Aaron, is that the money itself was meaningless. My self-respect is not measured in dollars. My choice was between letting go of my money or letting go of my self-respect. . . . Ask yourself this. If I gave you one hundred thousand dollars right now, would you be willing to spend four months in jail?"

I was getting an earful and did not respond to what I knew was a rhetorical question.

"You'd have to think about it, wouldn't you? It's *you* who came to believe my money represented freedom, not me. Remember to look at something from every angle before you go ahead and impose your values on someone else. And don't you see, that is exactly what you were doing?"

"Oh, my God, life truly is a paradox."

"Those are *my* words, Aaron."

"Yes, I know, you've always said that to me. But I'm beginning to think I see what you mean. It's almost like going to prison helps you appreciate what freedom really is . . . being in the closet can help you better understand what pride in yourself really is. . . ."

"Losing a parent can help you understand how important having one really is."

"So then it's these contrasts that help us grow?"

"It would seem so, my son. Life is a paradox. I'm not saying you should stop trying to figure it out, just keep this in mind as you do. Perhaps you'll find the greatest paradox is that there is no paradox. The possibilities are limitless."

"Dad, if you had only one sentence to describe what we've accomplished by writing this book, what would you say?"

"Gee, Aaron, I don't know. You're the writer, what do you think?"

"I've got some kind of block in summing it up. It's not that I'm at a loss for ideas, it's more like I have too many. I know we've accomplished a lot, but when I try to put it into words, I get tongue-tied, or brain-tied, or whatever."

"Well, one thing's for sure, Aaron. Once the book is published, we will have achieved immortality together."

I turned to him stunned, and he added, "Just kidding Aaron. That was a joke."

"No, Dad. I've learned that immortality doesn't come from books for homosexuals, nor is it exclusive to artists. Anyone who follows their heart can, and in that act does, achieve immortality. . . . You'll never guess who taught me that."

"Who?"

"You did, Dad. You did."

Then suddenly it occurred to us that the beauty of what we had accomplished was in the simplicity of the walk itself. The book was finished at that very moment; the last chapter had been lived.

"The great things of life are what they seem to be, and for that reason, strange as it may seem, are often difficult to interpret. But the little things in life are symbols. We receive our lessons most easily through them."

—*Oscar Wilde*

EPILOGUE

by Aaron

I could not have known that the last walk we took while in the process of writing this book would be the last walk we would ever take.

I returned to California and had the book finished by the spring of 1989. My plan was to save money until Christmastime, when I would reunite with my father in Rhode Island and we would go about getting our book published during the new year. On October 17, 1989, I happened to be in San Francisco when a jolting 7.1-magnitude earthquake struck. My father called me there on the eighteenth, greatly concerned for my safety. He was relieved to hear that I was fine. He did not mention his own health at all.

The next day, Thursday, October 19, he complained of serious internal pains and his doctor admitted him to the Rhode Island Hospital, with a foreboding, "You are a very sick man, Mr. Fricke." By Monday, October 23, his doctors still had not discovered the nature of his problems. When I spoke to him that day, he was not only coherent but characteristically indignant with his doctors for "taking their sweet time about this."

It was Tuesday, October 24, that everything changed. The doctors found a growth in his pancreas and diagnosed it as cancer. At sixty-two, my father had only a few months to live. At twenty-seven, and after seeing so many young people succumbing to AIDS, I had given more thought to questions about my own mortality than I had to his. I was not at all prepared.

I didn't know what to think, much less what to say when I called him that night. It scared me that the only strength I had to offer him was in the form of prayers. His voice was strained and he was breathing heavily in the brief time I spoke to him. His medication had been increased and I wasn't sure he understood everything I was saying. When I asked him whether the medication was easing the pain, I'm pretty sure he said, "A little." When I told him I was coming home right away and we would get our book published, he responded with a faint, "Oh, okay." Then I just said, "I love you, Dad." That he heard, and he responded with a little more energy. "Thank you. I love you, too, Aaron."

This was the last conversation we ever had. By the time I arrived in Rhode Island four days later, he was in a coma. I held his hand and noticed something I had never seen so clearly before: Our hands were almost exactly alike. I guess I just had not held his hand very much since the time I was a little boy. I put our hands in an overlapping position with one hand grabbing the other just above the wrist. He had demonstrated this grasp for me when I was young, saying it was the tightest grip you could get. He took me to the circus back then and told me that was why the trapeze artists used it. He said this was also the grip to use when pulling someone

out of the water if they fell overboard. I think in some way I was using this grip in the hope that it would pull him back, but it was no use; he had no grip. He was going.

My father died two days later, on October 30, 1989. I looked back out at Rhode Island and felt a cross between being totally lost in a place I had spent my whole life and totally at home in a place I had never been. Life took on the properties of a dream. I guess it had to. It was more than confusion; it was emotional chaos. Only twelve days earlier he had called me, worried about my safety. Now, by sheer coincidence one year plus four days since I had initially returned to Rhode Island to finish this book with him, he was gone.

I wondered, Can he really be gone? The question seemed as absurd as asking, Was he ever really here? I did not want to believe that in one breathtaking moment he had become part of my past, and never again would be part of my present or future. I wanted just one last chance to sit with him. Within weeks, I received that chance in a dream. He was sitting across the table from me in a restaurant, just as real as ever. He was looking through his wallet at things like his business cards and driver's license, and he said to me, "This is what I was," with an all-knowing kind of calm. He pulled a newspaper clipping out of his wallet, his obituary. When he read it aloud, he came across the date of his death and casually remarked on how it already starts to get cold by that time of year. He saw that I was crying, and when he reached out to comfort me, he disappeared into me. I woke up feeling that my father is part of me, and he always will be.

I decided that I would stay on the East Coast and go about getting the book published on my own, as I had been planning to return in December, anyway. Had things gone as planned, my father would have been with me to meet my agent and go on interviews; but as things turned out, I held on to this book and all the work he put into it, knowing in my heart that he was right by my side, after all. With that, I found the strength and determination to get this book published.

But, alas, this book must end with my father's passing. I considered mentioning this in the introduction, but that would have changed the entire meaning of the book. The book was not an afterthought and it was meant as a testament to life, not to my father's death. Everything except the words you are now reading in this epilogue was read and approved by my father. If some of the structure has changed, the ideas have not.

Most of the material that is not part of the reciprocal sections was finished by me and sent to my father for approval several months before he died. He returned this material to me with his comments in the margins. I incorporated these marginal comments into the text of the book. For instance, in reference to our conflict over my tardiness while writing this book, I originally claimed to have arrived at the worktable at 12:38 P.M. and sat down at 12:41 P.M. He crossed out both these times and substituted them with 12:54 and 12:57 P.M. Since the final editing was done after my father's death, we had to reach a tacit compromise on this one. In the final version, the times read 12:44 and 12:48 P.M. Most of my father's changes to this work were in a similarly minor vein.

In effect, my father continued to give shape to this book even after his death. His greatest contribution to it occurred during his lifetime, however. It contains his thoughts. Knowing that they may reach others as they reached me gives me a sense of peace. Our book was intended to be a book about two human beings, so even though my dad was not exactly a wealth of inspiration regarding homosexuality, he was able to give something much more important to this book—his humanity. He knew, as I do, that his greatest contribution was simply his effort and willingness to write it. That spoke more than all the words in this book.

Yet it is this book that I have left now. I cannot help but wonder what I would have felt had I not resolved that a reconciliation with him was imperative. Would I have been full of regret for the rest of my life or would I have found some distorted way to rationalize my lack of action? I thank God I will never have to answer this question. We always hope that we will do the right thing, but it is so rare that any proof of having done so will come screaming back. (More often, this happens when we do the wrong thing.) I am tempted, at this point, not only to critique this work but also what it represents in my life. That is not the book my father and I wrote, so I will refrain. Suffice it to say that with the help of my dad, I was given the opportunity to do the right thing. Thanks, Dad.

Two months after my father died, my sister and I carried out his last wishes to receive a burial at sea. My father's colleagues at Northeast Marine Pilots made the pilot boat available to release his ashes. As we sailed to Beaver Tail Point at the entrance to Narragansett Bay, I saw the Rhode Island shoreline creep by—a sight my father had seen count-less times—and despite the crashing waves and roaring wind, there was silence. It was the silence of memory. It is my memory; it is my father's memory.

As I write this, I can hear my father's response to it: "Oh, c'mon, Aaron, cut the melodramatics."

In all fairness, Dad, you deserve that last word.

Aaron Fricke
Summer 1990